Town Gardens

IMAGINATIVE IDEAS FOR "DIFFICULT" GARDENS

AREND JAN VAN DER HORST

INTRODUCTION BY RICHARD ROSENFELD

REBO
PRODUCTIONS

© 1995 Zuid Boekprodukties, Lisse
© 1996 Published by Rebo Productions Ltd
text: Arend Jan van der Horst
design: Ton Wienbelt, The Netherlands
photography: Marieke Uiterwijk, TextCase
Edited by: Richard Rosenfeld
translation: Stephen Challacombe for First Edition Translations Ltd,
Cambridge, Great Britain
typesetting: Fairfield Systems for First Edition Translations Ltd

ISBN 1 901094 36 7

Contents

Introduction

Town gardens are amazingly important. Not just as small green oases, but because they lend themselves to so many styles. Country gardens nearly always end up as a kind of pastiche. Of Vita Sackville-West, and Gertrude Jekyll, and even Rosemary Verey, who famously designed Elton John's garden. They end up as a homage to history. They are ensnared by the dreams of the past, by the garden 'rooms at Hidcote in Gloucestershire, by Versailles, by 17th century topiary, the incredibly neat, lace-like Baroque parterre, and by lofty Edwardian stateliness. But town gardens...

Town gardens often have the luxury of sitting in a cacophony of modern architecture with high-rise, glass fronted, shapes. Angular, thrusting and shiny. You can certainly create a cottage rural retreat, tucked away in the mayhem, and I've seen several in New York, but there's another exciting option. Create a modern garden using the same kind of materials as used by todayís leading architects. There is no reason why town and city gardens, small though they are, should not be modish and challenging and smart. Whichever style you prefer, the old, the known and the cosy, or the new, or even a mix of the two, Arend Jan van der Horstís book will help you. There is a good strong international flavour with ideas from Holland and Belgium, and France and Italy. Practical imaginative ideas like dragging big solid branches home from the wood, and using them to make rustic steps. And I love his idea of making great big circular apple trees, training them round large metal hoops, with pink-flowering roses beneath.

The art of gardening is before you do anything else, visit great gardens, in all styles, see what they do, the latest ideas, and then reinvent them back home, on a smaller, domestic scale. Town Gardens helps you do just that. It describes the internationally famous clematis collection at Burford House in Hereford and Worcester, where clematis are used as climbers, and amongst the ground cover plants. As Arend Jan van der Horst says, "This is virtually unknown anywhere else and is an excellent way to show them off." He is also quick to spot the clever, inventive way in which the French Count of Noailles trained a row of Cercis siliquastrum, the Judas tree, along a pergola, producing "a magnificent canopy of magenta blossom." Not something you see every day.

Town gardens are too easily, too snobbishly slandered, and ignored as second best. As places that can't quite make it. Dreadful, impoverished impostors. But most of today's top garden designers, especially those in America, are doing their best work in towns. I have seen roof balconies filled with bamboos and grasses, framed with walls of evergreens, and softened with collections of roses. Roof gardens that, if it weren't for the view – shooting across central London – would look like gardens on country estates.

Town Gardens is an excellent and timely reminder that small urban need not be second best. That, despite being squashed in by other buildings and all too often long and thin, they can, with just a few telling imaginative ideas, quickly become stunning, restful, and fun.

Richard Rosenfeld, East Sussex, 1996.

Tranquillity in the green garden

Those who live in a busy town know that pressures sometimes become too great so that there is a need for peace and tranquillity. Sometimes this is found in a spacious park with mature trees.

Sometimes peace can be found in a stately museum with high ceilings and quiet galleries displaying absorbing works of art. Or perhaps it can be found emanating from a house with long cool passageways and blinds that cut large windows down to size.

Then again, and surprisingly often, people walk out of the house into a shady garden surrounded by mature trees. The sound of traffic is distant, rather like strange abstract music. Birds sing, the sunlight is diffused, a breeze rustles gently through the leaves, and in the distance a lounger beckons. These oases of peace are generally found in older, to some, rather old-fashioned gardens, where there are no modern garden gimmicks but instead trees, *Rhododendron, Aucuba,* and grass.

The new inhabitant is often too quick to decide that the garden is dull and past it and allows the landscape gardener to disturb the peace with white paving slabs, wooden sleepers, and an axe. It is more sensible to see what can be added, by way of beautiful plants which thrive in shade and can update the garden, turning the once boring into a place of exciting beauty.

The perfect solution in such cases is often to supplement the existing planting with white and green plants, which are naturally suited to shady gardens.

The blue-grey colour left is Ruta graveolens, *which highlights the greyish theme of this old-world garden.*

5

Green with pale yellow or white flowers

There are many popular plants with pale yellow or white flowers. Some are shrubs, others are annuals, and there are also perennials and trees. Which were the trees that used to be planted in those pleasant old-fashioned leafy-green gardens and look so fine in maturity? Chestnut was a favourite because of its splendid white blossoms in spring and the large decorative green leaves. People did not worship the sun in those days and a pale complexion was considered fashionable. Consequently a summer-house with three sides open to the garden was a common feature. There the occupants could sit protected from falling blossom, leaves, and chestnuts. They were not concerned about the coarseness of the tree and only a few flower-beds were filled with roses and begonia tubers; the rest had lilacs, golden rain, rhododendrons, holly, and conifers to provide green in winter. Occasionally *Catalpa* trees are found in old town house gardens, suggesting this combination of white blossom and large oval leaf was popular in the last century.

More usually, we find apple and pear trees in town gardens. Pears grow tall but remain otherwise compact, whereas apples spread gracefully but are generally less tall than pears. Those who want a restful green and white garden will benefit from the blossoms of these fruit trees – white for pears and pink for apples – and then of course there are the fruits. They are a bonus which used to be very highly valued. Old-fashioned cooking pears were high on the list of favourites

Grey Senecio *grows against a wall; behind the cube of box can be seen grey* Stachys byzantina.

6

This eye-catching border has many grey-foliage plants mixed with green-leafed perennials. The result is an atmosphere that is silvery and airy. In the foreground is Stachys, *behind is* Artemisia.

and many preserving jars would be filled with their harvest. People also dried pears in their attics so they could enjoy them during the winter. In addition to the chestnut, *Catalpa,* and the fruit trees, there are many other white-blossoming trees that belong to the Victorian style. One is the acacia, which was chosen for its thin leaf, rapid rate of growth, and sweet smelling blossom. In those days it was invariably the successful *Robina pseudoacacia.* The white-flowering may is also found in town gardens, grown mainly as a shrub trained to create playful forms with the branches.

In many older gardens, white-blossoming lilac has been trained to form beautiful small trees with whimsical twisted trunks. Few ornamental apple trees were planted because of the preference for edible fruit. However, clouds of white blossom conjured up by *Malus floribunda* can occasionally be seen. The wide choice available is clear when we think of such small trees as the medlar *Mespilus germanica,* the quince, or the pocket handkerchief tree, *Davidia involcrata.* These are "old-fashioned" trees with white blossom. Frequently these trees of varying height were combined with large copper beech and columnar conifers to provide vertical contrast. Cedars were not common then in town gardens, though *Chamaecyparis lawsoniana* and varieties of *Thuja, Picea,* and *Abies* were.

This picture of tall trees and conifers was completed by a dense, predominantly evergreen under-planting of shrubs and dwarf conifers.

This white-themed back garden was created using Rosa 'Maria Mathilda', Anaphalis *and white* Dicentra. *Blue can be found in the lavender and the garden furniture which was specially painted in a shade of lavender.*

7

Shrubs and dwarf conifers

There are many shrubs which are typical of the gardens of our forefathers. Now many are available in varieties with dwarf habit and are longer flowering and have a greater assortment of colours than the shrubs of the past. Consider the mock orange *Philadelphus coronarius*, which envelops the entire garden in a cloud of white blossom. A height of at least 3m (10ft) was normal for this shrub which requires ample space. Plants used to be given sufficient room and their flowering times were chosen so that there was always something in bloom. Earlier than jasmine were a number of other shrubs, commencing usually with *Magnolia*, of which *Magnolia kobus* is an example. *Magnolia stellata* is another; it is a slow growing shrub. *Magnolia soulangiana* 'Alba Superba' is a white-flowering variety with the more common pink tulip-shaped flower. White flowering *Rhododendron* often flowers simultaneously with *Magnolia*. *Rhododendron* 'Catawbiense Album' is a white-flowering variety which grows wild, whilst R. 'Madame Mason' is a cultivated type. There are many more white-flowering varieties which can be distinguished at a glance. Sometimes they are pure white; and some have touches of green, black, or brown.

Nicotiana langdorfii is of upright habit. This 'Lime Green' example mirrors its name precisely.

Mollis azaleas and Knap Hill-Exbury azaleas are graceful shade lovers which our grandparents rejected. Mostly they preferred the soft pink varieties but for all that they knew of white types, such as azalea 'Persil.' White camellias are rarely seen because they are not hardy yet there are some town gardens with these white flowers which appear on evergreen shrubs. There are also much better-known shrubs which, in addition to azaleas (which are *Rhododendron),* put in an appearance. One is *Deutzia,* which was never absent from older town gardens. The previously mentioned *Aucuba, hollies, Kalmia,* and all sorts of dwarf conifers ensured a rustic, soft effect to blur the boundaries of the garden. Golden yellow was interchanged with green for vivid effect.

Roses

Roses were prized in the white-green garden, although our forefathers preferred pink and yellow-flowering roses planted in circular raised beds. White is preferred by the modern gardener. *Rosa* 'Iceberg', which is as a favourite cluster-flowering rose, is a large flowering white rose which displays just one huge bloom per stem. Then the other buds appear, swelling alongside the first flower.

The reawakened vogue for standard roses, which create fine effects to create different levels, is nice to see.

Climbing roses were extremely popular in the past, particularly against a pink or white background: there were climbers on trellises, over arches, summer-houses, and against fences. Double roses were popular. Large-flowered roses were used for bouquets or instead one bloom received full attention in a crystal or silver specimen vase. These days we plant such repeat-flowering specimens as *Rosa* 'Bantry Bay', 'Zepherine Drouhin', 'Compassion' (all violet), or *Rosa* 'New

Dawn' (soft pink). R. 'Albertina' is salmon pink and R. 'Climbing Iceberg' and R. 'Swan Lake' take care of the white effect. Yellow did not belong in the old-fashioned garden, though the older botanical varieties, which initially flowered fully and then grew exuberantly, are very pretty.

Old climbing roses   In ancient gardens, old climbing roses originating from long ago can be discovered. Josephine de Beauharnais, the first wife of Napoleon, had a large collection which she had recorded by the court artist Eduard. It can be seen in the Redouté rose museum known as L'Hay-les-Roses, to the south of Paris. These old varieties can still be obtained. There are white climbing roses such as 'Wedding Day', 'Bobble James', *R. filipes, R. multiflora,* and cream-coloured ones such as 'Blush Noisette.' Buy one or two and let them clamber where their tendrils can grasp hold of something. Put them against a trellis or train them along a wire, in old fruit trees, against a mimosa *(Acacia),* or against a garden shed.

Perennials such as lady's mantle *(Alchemilla),* variegated deadnettle *(Lamium galeobdolon* 'Variegatum'), and Christmas rose *(Helleborus)* fit in these gardens; as do white hortensias *(Hydrangea),* particularly in shady spots, and white varieties of hostas, *Hosta undulata.* Of the annuals, *Nicotiana* and *N. sandeae* 'Lime Green' can be utilized.

Above the neat hedge, there is a luxuriant world where the white Centranthus *has self-seeded, or perhaps there has been a helping hand.*

Wild plants or formal style?

A garden must not be entirely wild or entirely formal. Combinations are possible, and these can be very fascinating.

In this Italian garden, the round forms lighten and punctuate the evergreen hedges, setting a rhythm against which the light can play.

When I set about arranging my town house garden, the budget was not unlimited. The house was rented and people generally do not spend money on expensive planting for rented property. Instead I visited woods owned by a friend; there ivy climbed to the tree-tops. After I had pulled lengths of it from the trees and collected them in a plastic bag, the scions were planted in my garden, which is now a sea of ivy. Even the 15m (50ft) high walls of my right-hand neighbour's house are totally covered with it. Iron arches and obelisks are festooned with ivy and every tree acts as a climbing pole for the rampant growth. You must, of course, have the owner's permission before following this example.

Wild plants   Success with wild plants is assured provided the aspect of the garden is not too sunny, but even then it is usually no problem. Proof of this can be seen along verges and embankments of roads, which are home to numerous wild plants. Most garden centres stock these plants.

If the soil of your garden is naturally good or has been improved then the choice of wild plants is considerable. Lesser periwinkle (*Vinca minor*), variegated deadnettle *(Lamium galeobdolon)*, and bedstraw *(Galium odoratum)* – sometimes known as *Asperula odoratum* – are well-known wild plants which act as ground cover. There are also taller wild plants such as marguerite (*Chrysanthemum frutescens,*

10

synonymous with *Argyranthemum frutescens)* which are sun lovers, as are Cichorium, yarrow *(Achillea millefolium)*, and wild mallow *(Malva)*.

For damp spots there are some spectacular wild plants such as the yellow flag *(Iris pseudacorus)*, marsh marigold *(Caltha palustris)*, the arrowhead *(Sagittaria)*, purple loosestrife *(Lythrum salicaria)*, and the large ground-covering *Petasites hybridus*.

When choosing wild plants it is important to first decide what effect you want and to ascertain whether your garden is sunny or dry, or if there are any other growing conditions which need to be considered.

Dry soil: a disadvantage that can be turned to good use

Study of dry places in the natural environment shows what is possible. Common stonecrop *(Sedum acre)* is to be found in the driest spots and will happily thrive on red-hot flat roofs in summer. With this in mind, it can safely be planted between the joints of the patio or in plant containers which tend to dry out, and also beneath other drought lovers that provide ground cover. The flowering season for the blooms, which resemble little yellow stars, is long. Throughout the Mediterranean countries there are many examples of wild plants that thrive in dry sites, for example lavender *(Lavendula)*, thyme *(Thymus vulgaris)*, red valerian *(Centranthus ruber)*, and the rock rose *(Helianthemum)*.

This garden is formal, which is appropriate for the type of house. Roses bloom in compartments shaped like slices of a pie.

11

In Italy, yellow species of this plant can be found flowering in walls or between rocks in many places and anywhere stony. Pinks *(Dianthus)* grow as wild plants in these countries. Look for the dwarf types or the really tall ones such as 'Dalmatian pink.' To be practical, it is sensible only to choose plants which are similar to those known to cope with your local conditions. Marguerite, poppy, and sea kale *(Cramba maritime)* will survive in dry conditions, as will thrift or sea pink *(Armeria maritime)*, blue *fescue (Festuca glauca)*, and wild heather *(Calluna vulgaris)*. The choice is wide, dependent upon the desired end result. Plants can be grown from seed or bought from nurseries specializing in wild plants. Of course no protected species of plant should ever be taken home from the wild to your garden, and to protect the environment you should not simply help yourself to any plant.

Loosestrife, in the foreground (Lysimachia nummularia), *is one of the moisture-loving wild plants that can be easily cultivated.*

Moisture and sun lovers

Purple loosestrife and valerian like damp places as well as sunny ones, as does meadowsweet *(Filipendula)*. Yellow flag enjoys a sunny spot yet also thrives in shade. *Petasites hybridus* is happy with sun and moisture and grows rampantly wherever its roots find space. It is prudent to create a level area for it or the effect will be a chaotic wilderness. Mown grass, wooden boards, brick pavers, or gravel are all suitable provided they appear natural. Choose dark colours, or let plants self-seed themselves if using gravel so that no hard lines are visible between planting and gravel.

Shade and moisture

Many ground-cover plants such as *Vinca, Galium,* knotweed *(Polygonum bistorta)*, and ferns, like damp shade. They will grow in normal conditions but will not thrive as well, and this is particularly noticeable in dry summer months. How they cope with dry periods is directly dependent upon their position. They have no problem with such large shrubs as hazel, may, and medlar because these do not draw every last drop of moisture out of the surrounding ground. Large trees, however, absorb enormous amounts from the ground, sucking up gallons of water every day during sunny spells to feed their leaves. Consequently in such dry ground under trees, only ivy and the male fern *(Dryopteris filix-mas)* are able to survive.

Shade and drought

A beech wood that is as dry as a cork on a summer's day can be home to a rich kingdom of plant life. The principle can be applied in the garden by piling up brick pavers with rich soil behind them. The bricks retain moisture in their porous structure of fired clay. Moisture is absorbed during the night and from periods of rain. This enables plants to grow in deep dry shade. Deadnettle *(Lamium)* and all other plants specified for shade such as *Helleborus, Polygonum,* ferns, and ground ivy are able to grow in these conditions. There is a grass, *Festuca,* which thrives in shade and can cope with the wilderness beneath trees. Some requirements have to be met though. Only use it where the wind can blow away the leaves that fall. Rake off the leaves regularly or make a small slope so that they blow or fall away.

Moss, an oriental beauty

The result of thorough raking can be the creation of a soft green felt-like carpet. This is always possible under trees if the leaves are raked off. This evergreen moss can be walked on and instils a sense of calmness. The Japanese have venerated moss for centuries as something of beauty.

Take a light rake, preferably of plastic or bamboo, so that the earth is not disturbed. Moss occurs where large raindrops, falling for instance from trees, create a hardened layer of soil. This layer becomes sealed so that virtually no oxygen can penetrate the soil. All other weeds give up their attempts and moss, which has no roots but grows on the soil, seizes its chance. Accept the beauty and, after that raking, enjoy the felt-like green result.

The family who live at this town house frequently sit out on the patio of concrete pavers. Beside it, as intimate screening, is a white-yellow flower garden, featuring Rosa *'Iceberg.'*

Playful formality

Old engravings illustrate formal gardens of the seventeenth, eighteenth, and nineteenth centuries. Neat spaces with an occasional tulip, *Fritilleria imperialis*, marigold *(Calendula)*, or lily formed the planting. Edges of grass framed them to provide a pleasant view during the winter. There was no sumptuousness, instead there were large open spaces between the plants, which were partly perennials and

partly bulbs and annuals. Plants in pots were part of this scene, such as orange trees, laurels, *Agapanthus*, and *Pelargonium* from the Cape of Good Hope, which were extremely popular. The walls of town gardens were used in a practical way, to grow grapes and espalier fruit trees such as apple and pear, or there would be a hedge of hornbeam. If the garden was large, in the seventeenth and eighteenth centuries they would probably have created a beech arbour or bower. These were usually constructed from oak, formed into arches which were set about 2 to 3m (6 to 10ft) apart on each side and also at the rear. Beech was trained over this framework.

Prince Maurits had such a garden created for his castle, the Binnenhof, at the Hague. Jacques du Cerceau, a French artist of the seventeenth century, recorded for posterity in his precise engravings the way the French constructed huge walled gardens, which were then scaled down for imitation in towns at that time. All these elements can still be put to good use.

When I was once restoring a beautiful town garden, an arbour made of iron hoops was uncovered. It was replanted with old-fashioned varieties of roses. A nice touch was that at its centre there was a crown that had been formed out of iron tubing. This gave a festive finish to the rose arbour.

In the eighteenth century, box hedges (*Buxus*) were introduced to French gardens. They were hardy, easy to maintain and would grow for generations. Prior to box, hedges of hyssop (*Hyssopus officinalis*), lavender, rosemary, thyme and, *Santolina* were used, which are so much more interesting than the ubiquitous box. Hyssop produces blue flowers and is semi-evergreen; lavender and rosemary are both evergreens with blue flowers, though rosemary has grey-green foliage and twigs; whilst thyme, which is also evergreen, is pink to purple dependent on which variety is chosen. *Santolina* is very light grey and if trimmed into a hedge will not readily flower unless clipping is left until after flowering. In addition there is also *Teucrium*, which provides an evergreen hedge with pink flowers. All these species were used in my own knotgarden. The knot-garden is a sixteenth- to seventeenth-century style of garden. The patterns used for my modern version came from a seventeenth-century gardening book written by Jan van der Groen, who drew many designs which have been reprinted over and over again. The patterns of the hedge combine with each other so that, like knots in a rope, one hedge loops over the other.

In this border the plants are grouped effectively round a spacious lawn that catches the eye.

Box, the indestructible evergreen Since royal gardeners experimented with box for hedges in the seventeenth century for the enormous town gardens of the Louvre, the plant has become a permanent element chosen for many gardens.

15

Fashions come and go and there were periods between 1750 and 1900 in which formal gardens suffered mass slaughter, but fortunately a few saw the beauty of orderly arranged hedge patterns. Once again box is finding favour and being used to outline beds full of roses, herbs, or perennials; it is also used for individual examples of topiary, sometimes in pots.

Box can be purchased from almost any garden centre and new ways of using it are constantly being discovered. The following examples are suitable for use in town gardens.

Cornus canadensis.

Spheres

Spheres or balls of box can be combined at different levels as the starting point for a town garden. They provide pleasant interest to look out at in the winter, particularly when covered in frost or snow, and they become eye-catching as they grow larger.

Group them on both sides of the patio, or purposefully asymmetrically, for instance one or three spheres to one side of a terrace or path and three or five on the other. A line of spheres behind each other is an ideal way to suggest depth. They work well as sentinels around a circular lawn, surrounded by perennials and roses. In the summer these box forms provide a peaceful rhythmic element and calming foil for the exuberance of other plants.

Square forms

It is necessary to be cautious with the use of squares. They are used to good effect in the white garden at Sissinghurst in Kent, where they provide a calm focus for the grid of white-flowering, silver-leafed perennials, annuals, and occasional shrubs.

For a flower garden I once designed, I used squares to provide a point of visual rest. The multi-coloured flowers were divided into compartments, with a cube of box between every four compartments.

Topiary

Topiary can provide a fantasy element, but be careful not to overdo it. Understatement is more effective for the sophisticated gardener than fussiness. I have successfully used pots of "chickens" in a white garden, and I often place peacocks and chickens in rose gardens.

It is even possible to put them amidst the maze of perennials, where they are amusing and break up the regular shapes of a formal garden.

Scillas can be guaranteed to spread.

The form you choose should be dependent on the style of your house and its surroundings. A centuries-old standard, regarded in some cultures as a symbol of heaven, is four identical squares with either a circle or square at the centre. This was widely used in medieval herb and monastery gardens and it works just as well today.

For those living in a modern town house, it is a good idea to construct a formal herb, rose, or flower garden at the rear so that a peaceful area using lawn, water, and paving can be created between the house and the formal garden. For one modern house, a romantic back garden planted with entirely white flowers was designed (see diagram). Hedges were used to create drama and depth, whilst the siting of seating and pots gives the whole garden symmetry. The centre bed was at first planted with creeping camomile but has been changed to a pond with discs of stone over which water runs. A pleasing result has been achieved. To be really appreciated, the garden needs to be seen from the large windows of the living room, from the kitchen, or the study. Every view of the garden uses the changing light to provide constant variety.

Seen from the house

Next page: The "roof" which is formed by the balcony in this town garden has the advantage that you can continue to sit out during spring and summer showers.

1 terrace of grey concrete pavers

2 eight spherical *Catalpa* trees, *Catalpa bignoniodes* 'Nana', grown as standards

3 pond with stone edging

4 stone discs from which water falls into the pond

5 four spheres of yew (*Taxus bacatta*)

6 hardwood bench

7 yew hedge (*Taxus baccata*)

8 *Catalpa bignoniodes* 'Nana' trees, grown as standards

9 white roses, perennials, and hortensia (*Hydrangea*)

10 bench without back-rest in dark green

The patio garden

Those who want to keep maintenance to a minimum quickly realize that grass needs mowing every week during the summer. Large areas of lawn are not suitable for a low maintenance garden.

I designed this patio garden long ago. In the foreground is a raised wooden platform, then there are steps from sleepers with an area to sit on and for pots, and then (lower) a terrace of brick pavers. Behind is a wooded area with perennials.

These people should direct their attention to paths and areas paved with slabs, brick or concrete pavers, cobble-stones, or wooden planks. There is choice enough of materials to create an attractive patio garden.

Different levels for interest and variation

It is remarkable what difference a few steps up or down make to a garden, particularly if they cross from left to right of the centre line. This leads to a very interesting and surprising illusion of width which combats the natural elongated shape of most town gardens. The treads can be constructed inexpensively from hardwood or at greater cost from pressure impregnated softwood. Steps can be made of stone; about two-thirds of each "tread" is buried in the ground, leaving only one-third visible. This seems expensive, but properly mortared masonry will be more costly.

Steps of brick and cobbles

Where there is frost, masonry work requires a minimum foundation below ground of 2ft, Frost does not penetrate deeper than this into the ground and provided steps are properly constructed they should look fine for many years. Steps look best if they overhang the riser by 5 to 8 cm (2 to 3in). If you want a deeper overhang of say 10cm (4in), as was almost always the case in older gardens, then the material of the step must be at least 20cm (8in) thick. Such treads can be used in modern gardens but straight-edged treads are perfectly acceptable. Opt for no overhang so that the tread forms a neat right-angle. This particularly

suits concrete pavers. The joints look better if they are rubbed rather than pointed flush, so that the sun casts shadows for greater visual interest.

The area above and below steps will usually be paved in patio gardens, rather than grass. This can be cobbles, pavers, gravel, slabs, or even wood-chips.

Walls made of cobbles are usually built on fairly shallow foundations on sandy ground. On clay, peaty ground, or even good quality loam, proper foundations are essential, particularly if small cobbles are to be used. Large stones or pieces of rock might permit a wall to be built with minimal foundations but its life expectancy depends on the ground conditions and perhaps a little luck.

Steps from tree branches

It may seem absurd to use tree branches to build steps but it is cheap, and it is easy to drag them home. Ideally half of the thickness should be set into the ground, although this is not essential, Drive stakes in on either side of the "step" – where they will be hidden by plants – to prevent the branch from sliding. If bark is spread on the path it will provide the perfect basis for a rustic patio garden using wild plants. More often though, decorative plants are chosen and they are ideal for the notion of a "room outdoors."

In the foreground of this hotel is a dry-stone wall of flagstone kerbing. It is one of a number of different garden styles to be seen here.

**Low walls in the
outdoor room**

Raised beds can be built around the patio with edges wide enough to sit on. The rims of these beds need not be very broad though, and they can be hidden by an exuberance of vegetation.

Just like steps, raised beds and boundary walls of masonry need foundations 2ft deep, which is both costly and laborious. This is why many gardeners use wood for hard landscaping. Timber which is pressure impregnated is suitable, and tropical hardwood is ideal. Check though that the timber is from sustainable forests which are properly replanted, so that your purchase does not contribute to the destruction of the ecologically sensitive rain forests.

Drive sturdy impregnated poles into the ground. Poles of, for instance, 70cm (28in) need to go 30cm (12in) into the ground, so that about 40cm (16in) show above ground. The first plank should be set slightly into the ground and the top plank of those nailed to the poles can be finished with a capping, but that is not essential. In any event, make sure the capping does not stand proud since this catches the eye in an ugly way.

Walls of large boulders are somewhat overdone but walls made of rustic cobble-stones look very attractive with plants hanging over them. Bricks are fine – even imitation concrete "stones" and cobbles are suitable.

Plant shrubs around the patio to make the walls bright green in summer. Low walls divide the space and provide somewhere to sit or place a plant pot.

21

Natural stone walls   Our parents and grandparents loved real stone, such as flagstones. Stone has been making a comeback and many modern gardens are once again full of this material. Apart from flagstones, which are generally sawn straight, pieces of rock are available which can be used for dry-stone walls. These are mostly dressed or cut stone, or lengths which if required can be mortared together to form a wall. Each country and region has its own sources of stone of varying qualities and properties. If the choice is granite, darker varieties may be preferred or those with a rosy tint.

Sleepers: cheap and natural   Sleepers are ideal for buildings, walls, and steps. They lend themselves naturally to being piled up, they are pleasantly coloured, and provided attractive planting covers them they are perfectly acceptable and cheap. No foundation is necessary, although it is advisable to have the first sleeper dug into the ground.

Dry-stone walls   Dry-stone walls are a delightful feature provided they are overgrown with interesting plants such as the creeping thyme (*Thymus brittanicus*), periwinkle (*Vinca*), *Iberis,* and other creepers, The advantages of the dry-stone wall are three-fold. First, it allows you to achieve a natural overgrown look, Secondly, putting earth in the gaps in the wall enables plants to gain a foothold and flourish, and, finally, it is a cheap way to build a wall because no foundations are required.

A stout fence closes the garden off and turns it into a patio. Flagstones, small walls, and pots all work to create an intimate area near the house where it is always possible to add a plant or two.

A side step: slopes, walls and hollows

Every town garden, with or without a patio, can be made more interesting by creating different levels, using slopes, walls, and hollows which flow smoothly into each other.

Imagine a long town garden. From the French windows of the house a brick path gently slopes downhill and on either side of it there are perennials and ground-cover evergreens. Roughly half-way down the garden, the slope levels out and there are features such as a lawn, pond, and terrace.

At the back of the garden, all the soil that has been dug out has been placed so that a path climbs up with banks of earth on each side. These are planted with attractive shrubs – evergreens such as *Rhododendron*, holly, bamboo, and *Viburnum burkwoodi*. As a feature at the end of the garden a hedge is planted with three asymmetrically sited shrubs, which may or may not be evergreen. These could be three conifers of columnar form. To prevent the piled earth from being washed away at the borders of the garden, sleepers are piled on top of each other or a palisade of wooden pales is driven into the ground. The use of special membrane or agricultural plastic to resist root penetration behind the palisade prevents earth from trickling between the joints. The scope for variety with walls, hollows, and hillocks is endless. You can really use your imagination so that your garden can be a unique one-off.

Between this house and the summer-house I created two borders. This, the left-hand border, catches the morning sun. The path acts as a mowing edge.

23

For a restful green carpet plant Waldsteinia, Vinca *and* Pachysandra, *low maintenance ground-cover plants with yellow, blue, and white flowers respectively.*

Sometimes I design a garden with a round patio or lawn at the far end, surrounded at the side and rear by an earth bank. Halfway around this is planted a closely cut rounded hedge with trees and shrubs behind it.

In front of the hedge of perhaps yew are ground-cover plants for a maintenance-free garden, or perennials and roses for a colourful garden. Close to the house there is a semi-circular or fully round terrace with earth sloping uphill away from it. Here too are roses or ground-cover plants such as *Eupatorium, Lavatera,* and decorative grasses. Link this terrace with a grassy path or one of identical paving material to the terrace and the beginnings have been created for a town garden that is "natural" to the eye.

Try to retain as much sun as possible to keep the garden cheerful and inviting and to encourage many flowering plants to grow. For plenty of sun it will be necessary to leave the larger trees out of your planting scheme.

For ample colour you can choose between lots of bright colours or carefully considered drifts of colour and matching tints. The multi-coloured look is seen everywhere and for that reason it is less interesting. More exciting is bright colours with sophistication. Think about

At this restaurant slopes have been planted with Saxifraga *(saxifrage) which has such tiny flowers that they form a haze of pink.*

The vegetation in the patio garden

24

combining different shades of pink, violet, purple, blue, and white; or yellow, butter yellow with soft lemon yellow, orange, bright red and deep red. There is iris blue or forget-me-not blue, *Brunnera* – the perennial which flowers like forget-me-nots – flax (*Linum perenne*), and delphinium. Absolutely not multi-coloured but sensational is a garden of white roses, white and soft-green tobacco flowers (*Nicotiana* 'Lime Green'), and tall white delphinium.

Tall features It may be important to create a "green wall" as a boundary in order to gain maximum privacy. It is frequently difficult to get permission to build a wall or erect a fence. If your neighbours agree, you have one problem fewer when you create your extra "outdoor room." A length of wall on one side, an extension to the house, may be sufficient to give the closed "room" effect.

Further along from the house a dense evergreen hedge can do the trick. Tall dark-green netting overgrown with ivy is also effective, as is evergreen honeysuckle. To add a taller dimension plant a dwarf fruit tree and prune away its lower branches to keep the view unobstructed. This can also be done with lilac, decorative apple, pear, quince, medlar, or pollarded holly. If you want shade then a bower can be created by planting plane trees (*Platanus*) which during the winter have their branches trained horizontally to form a canopy.

Mahonia is an ideal plant for flower arrangers and for lazy gardeners. The shrub will grow almost anywhere, sun or shade, in damp or dry spots. The flowers are yellow and frequent, the leaves are shiny, and in the case of Mahonia aquifoleum 'Atropurpureum' they can be slightly reddish coloured.

25

Branches below 2.5m (8ft) are removed and the crowns of the tree are pollarded. The way in which the plane sheds its bark adds additional interest. It is easier to choose a tree which does not grow tall and has a natural ball shape.

May, elderberry, crab apple, pear, and all other types of fruit tree can be treated in this way to provide a green parasol. If cherry trees are used it is almost impossible to over prune them as they should be cut back frequently to stop them becoming too large.

An oriental green patio garden

Camellia is frequently used in Japan to create some height in their gardens, or they plant maple (*Acer palmatum*), and pine (*Pinus*), that needle-rich conifer which is easily trimmed to shape. Choose *Pinus cembra* or *Pinus parviflora*, because these naturally grow whimsically and open, so that only a minimum of cutting to shape is required.

Maple is available in many shrub varieties but do not choose any of the trees from this family because they will grow too large. *Camellia* is attractive but compact; prune them after flowering to limit their height. Should you want to let a shrub grow freely, then prune as lightly as possible but remove the innermost branches so that an airy shrub is formed which can be seen through.

A flowery patio with sun, grey-coloured paving, and grey-white plants. On the right is the tall Eupatorium.

A special little-known evergreen is *Nandina domestica* (heavenly or sacred bamboo). This Japanese shrub has bare branches and lance-shaped leaflets which stick out horizontally. The feathery white flowers which it produces in spring and summer are succeeded by translucent and decorative red fruits.

Impatiens glandulifera

Because Japanese gardeners are fond of trimming and cutting plants to shape, they plant trees which can be kept small by careful shaping and pruning. *Gingko biloba* is such a tree. It is a very ornamental example of needle-bearing conifer whose needles grow into spatula-like leaflets. They change colour from green to golden-yellow in autumn. They are pruned after the leaves have fallen, or sometimes before (I have seen that done in the streets of Tokyo). This is done to stop the leaves falling. In Japan the tree is usually kept at a height of about 3m (10ft) and in a columnar shape. This is because it is planted in the busy shopping streets and the Japanese wish to keep its dimension as narrow as possible. The height is determined by overhead electricity cables. In the eastern patio garden in Japan, partitions consist of bamboo, grey or black trellis, or a hedge.

This shallow step using a sleeper divides the terrace from garden and ground-cover plants such as Campanula potenschlagiana.

A wall to form the boundary In the town garden, it is possible to build a surrounding wall to guarantee maximum privacy. This works well in practice and it gives the opportunity to use many climbing plants which are fragrant and long flowering.

In the garden in the diagram these are also used on the pergola, which acknowledges and repeats the symmetrical design and at the same time divides the lower garden in two. The sunken garden at the front also intentionally separates different areas of the garden and provides a place to view the garden from the partially roofed terrace near the house (1). Brick pavers have been used for paths and other hard surfaces. The garden colours are pink, purple, blue, and grey which pick out the colours of the paving and walls. The result is a warm-coloured garden with the areas of grass providing tranquillity. The walk to the summer-house is intentionally designed to cause the stroller to pause to look at what is currently in flower.

1 terrace with natural hard stone slabs

2 sunken pond with pewter ornamental fountain

3 sunken area of perennials and rose garden with lavender and *Rosa* 'The Fairy'

4 shady terrace beneath pergola; in reality it has become filled with many pots and a large birdcage

5 sun terrace beneath pergola with roses and wisteria

6 perennials in pink, blue, and grey hues

7 summer-house to draw the eye

8 the wall, which is 2.5m (8ft) high

Two beautiful features: water and topiary

Water and topiary both fascinate through the sensational effects they can create, ensuring there is no risk of a dull garden. I try to introduce both features into almost every town garden I design.

Water can mean a large pond covering more than half the garden or a small pond, from a garden centre, alongside the patio. A small pond will be a constant source of changing interest for anyone who sits by it. Sometimes I install one across the width of a garden so that a bridge is necessary to move from one part of the garden to the other.

Happily not every garden is filled with every imaginable species of plant in wide variety. This tranquil garden is relaxing with its pond and its sculpture by Miro.

Four good reasons to have water features in the garden

The most important reason for featuring water in a town garden is that water in an enclosed garden reflects the sky. All sense of being hemmed in vanish when there is a mirrored surface surrounded by ferns and ivy, lawn, perennials, and beautiful examples of topiary.
The second reason is that there are copious beautiful plants to arrange alongside a pond especially the large-leafed species such as *Ligularia, Hosta, Rodgersia Gunnera*, which look spectacular by the waterside. The somewhat lower growing bog plant *Lysimachia nummularia* is interesting as completely flat ground cover, with perhaps just a single meadowsweet pushing its way above it. *Waldsteinia ternata* is another plant to choose for low level ground cover; others are *Aceana, Vinca*, and *Euonymus fortunei* 'Carrieri.'

The third reason is that the life of the pond will bring great enjoyment. A pond gives its owner more than the delight of the many plants that thrive at the waterside; it attracts wild life to your garden. Birds drink

at the pond, there are frogs – if you value them – whilst water-boatmen and other insects skim the surface, water snails consume plant remains and for true nature lovers there are salamanders or newts, toads, and other water dwellers which can be bought and introduced to the pond. For children this is an exciting place to learn and it requires little maintenance provided a balanced ecology can be achieved.

The fourth reason is that a long garden can be sub-divided with the addition of a dramatic water feature which is a constant source of pleasure, so that sitting, looking, and strolling around such a garden becomes exciting.

What sort of terrace beside the water? The most interesting choice is wooden decking. Stain the timber black or allow the planks to weather to grey. Deal that is machined to provide a grip *is* less slippery than planed surfaces. Unseasoned and untreated timber resists algae growth longest. Fix the planks onto sleepers placed 60cm (24in) apart as bearers. It is best to use boards of a minimum 4cm (2in) thick. Thinner planks would require the distance between bearers to be reduced to avoid them bending. Square decking looks really good or, if there is sufficient space, decking sections can be placed alternately on one side and the other leading from the house to the pond. A long wooden path could lead from the house

The combination of water-lily leaves and the foliage of other perennials creates a unity of form. Here Hosta hangs down with Bergenia to ogle at dragon-fly, frog, and water-spider.

to a large area of decking. Where the deck is on the other side of the pond from the house, this leaves an undisturbed view of the pond from the house of whichever shape is chosen – square, round, elongated, or a natural looking free form.

Brick paving

Specially fired bricks are available for use with ponds. After a while moss gains a foothold on them and self-seeded plants take root so that a delightful transition from paving to pond is created. Allow the bricks to cover the lip of the pond, to bring about a secretive, shadowy surround which acts as a place for fish to hide from the neighbours' cats. Concrete paving bricks are the cheapest but they always look harsh, even in the shadows. They are more practical than fired clay bricks but less attractive, because they soon look drab. Now though there are new small concrete pavers, such as imitation cobble-stones, with a more natural, less obviously artificial finish. Their rough edges permit moss to gain a foot hold. Setts and pebbles are to be found in both granite and concrete, and these are ideal for pond surrounds. Alternatives include shingle or chippings, wood chips, and bark.

Materials for ponds

In the past clay was puddled or worked to seal the bottom of a pond. When filled with water it would be perfectly water-tight but there was one problem. Water-plants can take root in the bed of the pond and perhaps run rampant – which can be a particular problem with

This shape, which creates a sense of depth, lends itself to both swimming pools and ponds. The parasol enhances the effect by acting as an eye-catcher.

31

Those who do not wish to consider a pond, might choose a water trough or bowl. In this garden, old feeding troughs help to form a strong composition.

water-lilies. The roots of the plants are difficult to remove without damaging the waterproof layer. This is why concrete-bottomed ponds became more popular than clay ones. Concrete is an ideal solution, provided care is taken over two important points. The pool base must be reinforced with steel mesh set in the concrete and the pool sides must slope slightly outwards to let ice slide upwards. When water freezes, it increases in volume and many a concrete pool has been damaged by the considerable pressure which ice can exert. I experienced it once with a large, curved and meandering pond where the contractor was not willing to build sloping walls yet was prepared to guarantee upright ones. In that garden there were four enormous black-stained square timber decks behind the house, where the pond with its curved shape was crammed in on two sides. The other two sides were reserved for the plants – consisting of decorative grasses – deal from Austria, bamboo, and gravel – lots of gravel. Round concrete stepping-stones were placed throughout this Japanese-orientated world. One square deck was roofed over with glass-fibre, so that sitting out in the garden was less dependent upon the weather.

Plastic   Plastic is undoubtedly the most popular material for ponds because it is relatively cheap and simple to construct. Drive a stake into the ground every l to 1.5m (3 to 5ft) and screw or nail a hardwood board to them. The board must be perfectly level so that the pond edge will

This natural looking pond alongside a covered terrace has large groups of imposing green plants which create an imposing and tasteful garden.

also be level. The plastic liner is pulled over this frame. Each professional has their preferred way to finish off the edge of the pond. I fix a plank on the inside of the pond so that no plastic will be visible if the water-level should unfortunately fall. A batten fixed to the top of the frame ensures that no plastic is visible from above. The plastic can be clamped between two boards and the surplus that sticks out trimmed with a sharp knife. Let slabs or bricks slightly overhang the rim for an attractive finish. Where there will be planting, lay peat blocks over the edge of the pond. They too should slightly overlap, ideally sufficiently to touch the water. This brings about an attractive planting area at the water's edge for the many plants which like to put down their roots in moist ground.

In Japan Azaleas are trimmed into rounded sculptures after flowering.

To stop the blocks of peat falling in, perhaps through birds drinking and splashing at the water's edge, take measures as follows. One method is to place mortar behind the rim and to press an end of the block – usually about 20 to 25cm long (8 to 10in) into the mortar. Another way is to pin each block to the ground using metal or wooden tent pegs (not the sort with round ends). Wire netting stretched over the peat blocks has been used to hold them together.

Polyester   In Belgium, ponds are often made by using polyester. For a large private garden, two different but suitable methods can be utilized. The

The green balustrade of the bench echoes the wealth of greenery and grey plants in pots surrounding it.

first is to construct a base of concrete or block-work which need not be water-tight. The polyester pond is then fixed to this base.

For the other method a pond is dug out with sides sloping outwards at least 45 degrees. In a temperature only just above freezing on this occasion, polyester fibres were laid on top of each other. Constructing the edge of the banks is fairly easy. Sections of upright standing polyester fibre matting are stuck to the base and the area behind it is filled in with heavy soil. Once the water-plants are put in, the difficult part of building a pond is completed. Water-lilies are sunk to the bottom in weighted plastic or wicker baskets. The bottom needs to be at least 70cm (28in) deep. Experience proves this to be sufficient since water rarely freezes at this depth, leaving an area clear of ice in which fish can survive the winter.

In this somewhat dark garden there is a maze-like pattern of paths and hedges, with the occasional cube of hedge.

Getting to grips with topiary

People have clipped and trimmed hedges, pruned fruit trees, and reduced overgrown shrubs and trees to size for as long as there have been gardens. Nature has been controlled in the way man wills. In the early gardens of Egypt, Mesopotamia, and Greece there were functional reasons for pruning. There was a need to train grapes, for instance, and to keep peaches within reach so the fruit could be harvested. This need to determine the way a plant grew in the royal gardens and at the courts of the wealthy took on its own life. The merely

functional was changed to meet the ideal of creating beauty. Design became a gardener's art. At Pompei, under the layers of lava that snuffed out the city, delightful engravings have been found which give an insight into Roman tastes. A slave, known as the "topiaricus", maintained the hedges planted throughout the courtyard gardens of the town. Houses were often built around such a courtyard. The hedges were of rosemary or cypress, both of which species can cope with hot weather. Even in those days small trees and hedging were trimmed in special shapes such as spheres or layers, one above the other. Cones and suchlike were a sign of the topiarist's art.

Topiary was also widely used by Muslims for their enclosed gardens. In a Moorish garden in Granada, known as El Chapiz, four cypresses with their tops trained towards each other create a natural summer-house. This is just one of many good ideas for plants grown in our own climate. In Granada, topiary is the central feature of a rose garden.

In medieval gardens topiary was commonplace. Foremost was the layering of branches to form discs with space between them, cubes, and spheres. In baroque times, spirals became popular. The garden of the Het Loo palace in Apeldoorn, in the Netherlands, offers an excellent overview of topiary styles; as does the historical garden at Aalsmeer, also in the Netherlands, where all kinds of chickens,

When the neighbours started to get rather noisy, I cunningly created this fountain for my clients. It came originally from a cathedral. The sound of water splashing into the semi-circular pond is now the main source of background noise in the garden.

35

This garden was designed around the use of grass, decking, and giant coltsfoot. This wild plant needs to be kept in check but provided this is done, much pleasure can be derived from the round broad leaves and the clusters of early spring flowers which rise from the ground just after the snow.

peacocks, little bears, and spirals are set out for everyone to admire. Shrubs for topiary do best planted in the ground in fertile soil. When grown in pots, they need feeding with pig manure two or three times each year.

The way in which topiary is used in a garden will depend entirely upon individual requirements. Be careful to avoid anything excessive, for that can mar the effect intended for the garden. There are, however, many delightful town gardens in which topiary is an essential feature. I know one that has trees and shrubs which would otherwise be too large trimmed and shaped in all manner of forms. Spheres of yew, placed between the foliage of perennials surround a pond. In a herbaceous border of white and gold there are gold and silver varieties of multi-coloured privet, together with the silver *Cornus elegantissima* in spherical form, which acts as somewhere for the eye to rest as it traverses a host of perennials and annuals. In an iris garden, at one end there is a stone column apparently surmounted by the sphere of yew planted immediately behind it. More yew are formed into cones here and there to ensure interest in the garden even in winter. All of these ideas can be used in the town garden. In one example metal hoops were used to train apple, pear, and quince in an area which is filled with pink-flowering perennials and roses. In a colourful cut-flower garden, the garden is divided by espaliered lime trees from which

A wooden bridge virtually leads the way across the water. Behind it is Miscanthus sinensis 'Giganteus.'

emerges a peacock in yew standing on one foot. By the swimming pool are balls, chickens, and peacocks; and little bears formed in box stand in the grass. In a white garden consisting of six areas of perennials and roses surrounded by box hedges with a grass pathway between them, the centre of each compartment has a tall yew obelisk. Box spirals in pots are dotted about on the terrace. In the blue garden a box topiary form stands on one leg as the main focal point at the end of a grass path, and to either side broad borders are filled solely with blue-flowering shrubs and perennials. Where the scale permits topiary can be allowed full rein.

For many years, I cultivated a giant yew chicken in the garden of my own Amsterdam town house. It did not thrive in the poor, dry soil but slowly took shape. Topiary figures can take years if self-cultivated. There are even box topiary examples in my garden which are in the form of standards. This was an accident, however, when the undersides of my first attempts at creating cones in box went wrong and I was forced to remove the rather frayed lower branches. There are endless possibilities in the way that grapes, espaliered fruit, and plane trees and mimosa in shrub form can be pruned and trained. Topiary is also possible with simple shrubs such as privet, beech, and holly and with conifers such as yew, *Juniperus communis,* and *Chamaecyparis.*

This beautiful garden was designed after the Second World War by the Dutch landscape architect Rooyaards. I replaced the persistent floating grass Glyceria aquatica *with* Hosta tardiana 'Halcyon' – *which has a small blue leaf and* Hosta sieboldiana 'Elegans' – *which has a large blue leaf. The spirals of box are outstanding.*

The patio garden

In northern Europe it is unusual to see an enclosed courtyard patio at the front of the house. In this diagram such a feature provides an intimate courtyard to which to withdraw and a suitable place to cultivate figs, quince, and walnut. However, a fine specimen of birch stands in a suitable spot and has been allowed to remain there. The walnut is to the right of the rear of the house in the area divided by yew hedges into gardens for sitting, relaxing, and enjoying the pond.

A greenhouse acts as an orangery where it is glorious to tarry among the collection of orange trees, with a view of the long straight pond which flatteringly mirrors the white flowers on either side.

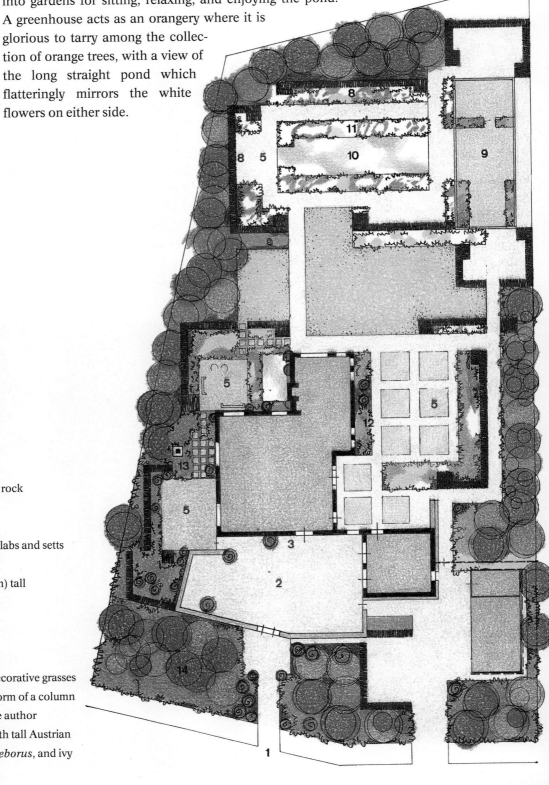

1   public road

2   courtyard with slabs of rock

3   front door

4   parking for car

5   paved areas of paving slabs and setts

6   walnut, existing

8   yew hedge 1.6m (5ft 4in) tall

9   terrace

10 pond

11 white garden

12 blue planting

13 green planting, with decorative grasses and a fountain in the form of a column of rock designed by the author

14 area of "woodland" with tall Austrian deal, ferns, birch, *Helleborus*, and ivy

Tasty delicacies from the garden

Almost every town garden has room for herbs and spices. Not only are they attractive and generally easy to grow, but they have additional uses.

In the most unfavourable situation, where there is almost total shade, you will not fail with varieties of mint which will prosper in front of shrubs.

One advantage of a shady site is moisture retention, causing luxuriant growth. There are varieties of mint which can be cultivated in pots. If the garden is mainly in shade but the patio is sunny, a few plants can be placed on the patio. Some varieties of mint, which are delicious in tea, ice-cream, or even yoghurt, are beautiful decorative plants. An example is *Mentha rotundifolia* 'Varigata', the small leaf of which is edged with white. It bears clusters of very light purple, almost white, flowers. The leaves are less dark in shade and the invasiveness which makes many varieties of mint problematical plants is not too serious. Variegated mint is ideal in front of *Rhododendron*, between Hosta, and alongside *Cimicifuga*.

To take a closer look at the mint family, the common kitchen herb is *Mentha spicita,* which has a strong scent and green leaves. *Mentha rotundifolia* is the white mint with a round, somewhat greyish leaf. There are also a number of varieties of this species with a cream-green leaf.

Peppermint is *Mentha piperita* in Latin. It has a metallic-green leaf and a strong spicy scent. There is a wide enough choice of varieties of

This is one way to dry onions. For those who would like to try, there are all kinds of delicacies to be made from the garden.

39

mint but *Mentha longifolia* 'Buddleja' has not yet been mentioned. This variety has a silver-grey leaf and I discovered it when wandering through the garden of Peter Baak at Eext in the north-eastern Dutch province of Drenthe. An intimate herb garden which I designed has been created there in a cloistered courtyard, complete with espaliered fruit trained to metal hoops.

A mint garden in the style of the cloister

The garden at Eext has numerous ideas suitable for the town garden. Creating arches around a part of the larger garden provides a means for fruit to gain some shade from the sun. In shaded gardens, the arches could be painted dark green and planted with honeysuckle, *Clematis,* or hops (*Humulus lupulus*). Of course there should be a path beneath the arches, preferably of brick or just firm soil.

Tropaeolum majus

Create a number of small beds for a mint garden because the plants are so invasive. This is why I sometimes advise placing each variety in a separate plastic pot with drainage holes at the bottom, to limit growth. An alternative is to create compartments surrounded by walls or some other hard barrier to encircle each plant – or corrugated plastic sheeting could be used. Bury this so that a ring of plastic 40cm (16in) deep surrounds the plants to prevent the roots creeping. Do not be surprised though if some runners feel their way over the barrier in search of new areas to colonize. At Eext, the plants in the mint garden are cut back each winter with a spade. The excess is sold to visitors to these gardens. Of course, neighbours and friends can benefit from a pot of mint as a present.

The mint beds in the cloister garden at Eext are set around the edge and also in the centre of the garden.

To provide winter interest, spheres of box are planted between the metal hoops. The owners set a huge potted laurel more than 2m (6ft) high in the centre of the garden as a beacon and tall focal point while the mint was not fully grown.

Mint recipes

Mint from the garden is delicious with tea. Put the mint in the pot with the tea before adding boiling water. The taste is spicy and distinctive, and far more delicious than the fashionable mango, lemon, and orange teas. To enjoy it in the winter, dry the stalks of mint. When they are truly dry, pull the crackling leaves off and put them in an airtight jar to store them without loss of scent or flavour. In addition to mint tea, which even the most useless gardening cook can make, there are plenty of other recipes.

In Britain, roast lamb is traditionally accompanied by mint sauce. Yoghurt is fantastic served with finely chopped mint, pieces of apple, and orange.

Elder as a shrub for the shady garden

There are many types of elder, including the wild species known in Latin as *Sambucus nigra* and the sort which has a fine feathered leaf and is known as *Sambucus racemosa*. Both thrive in the shade. Once one elder has blossomed and produced berries, the birds will distribute the seeds to the whole garden. Before long there are as many elder shrubs and trees as are needed to fill any bare patch in the garden. Make sure there is evergreen behind elder because it looks rather bare and uninteresting in winter with grey-brown stem or trunk. Permit ivy to climb up the larger trunks or for an attractive solution, plant evergreen honeysuckle (*Lonicera henryi*), which will prosper with the elder to climb up and looks beautiful in frost and snow.

Elderflower is a jewel that fills shady corners and sunny ones with light cream umbels – umbrella or parasol-like flower clusters. The berries are edible. One way to enjoy them is to peel and core some apples and then slice them thinly. Put the apples in the pan with one cluster of elderberries and one and a half tablespoons of water per apple (sufficient because of the moisture that comes out of an apple), add half a tablespoon of cane sugar per apple and let it cook to a pulp. Elderberries with stewed apple can be eaten hot or cold. For elder tea, dry the flowers so that the tea can be drunk in the winter as well as the summer. Use two teaspoons of dried elderflower per person. Pour boiling water on and allow to brew so that the flavour is developed.

Herbs and spices are necessary for the kitchen and also useful for driving away all kinds of unwanted creatures; try mint for flies Galium for moths. They are also delightful to behold, as in this well-stocked garden.

41

Elderflower fritters are also delicious. Make a light batter with flour, salt, sugar, and milk – similar to that used for apple fritters. Heat oil, sprinkle the elderflowers with cinnamon, and then drag them through the batter and fry them until crisp in the hot oil. Serve sprinkled with icing sugar.

Chives: even in partial shade

This grass-like plant known in Latin as *Allium schoenoprasum* is one of the most frequently used herbs. There are even restaurants named after it. An example is the one in an old fort in Purmerend, the Netherlands, called La Ciboullette, which is French for chives.

Chives need to be split after a year and the ground fed with manure if they are to remain vigorous and green in the overworked soil of a town garden. They will grow almost anywhere except in deep shade.

The ways in which I use chives are simple. Finely chopped lengths of chives are strewn over an omelette. Occasionally I serve egg with chives. Boil eggs in the usual way and allow them to stand in the hot water for ten minutes. Then cool briefly in cold water. Remove the shell but keep the egg whole, and place it in a warm glass so that the egg is upright. Season with pepper and salt, and sprinkle with finely chopped chives and serve with toast.

Dandelion, Taraxacum officinale

There are new vegetables already sown where the onions have been dug up.

When the word *officinale* is added to the name of a species, it indicates that the plant is useful. That can be as a medicinal herb in which the leaf, root, or some other part of the plant such as a seed or pod is used; or because it is edible as a flavouring or seasoning. The dandelion seeds blow in on the wind. If there are no plants in the garden due to high walls and you would like to grow them, then collect some of the seeds and cover them lightly with earth. They will grow in sun or partial shade.

In France the leaves are eaten in salads: pick them young and serve dressed with vinaigrette. Eaten with apple, they are delicious. To keep the leaves white and moist, cover the plants with a pot. A simple use is for tea. Pick young leaves and add a litre of water per 50g (2pt per 2oz) of dandelion leaves, bring to the boil and allow to stand for ten minutes. Sieve the liquid and serve with honey to sweeten. The real enthusiast will make dandelion wine by pouring boiling water over the leaves and leaving them to steep for ten days. Then add sugar and the zest of lemon and orange together with the peeled fruit. Allow this to warm through for about ten minutes and then leave to cool. It is delicious to drink.

Lovage thrives in partial-shade

This seasoning plant for soups and stews, *Levisticum officinale*, grows very tall in full sun and fertile ground. In the shady garden, the plant should be set towards the back of the border because the leaves

are unattractive. It is best to cut the plant right back from time to time. Old leaves can be dried or thrown away and the new leaves used. They are useful for seasoning soups, or in stock and stews – chop a small amount finely for a strong flavour.

Salad with carrot and lovage

Finely chop a carrot and an apple. Add two teaspoons of finely chopped lovage and mix this gently with yoghurt, mayonnaise, salt, and pepper. Wash an Iceberg lettuce and shake dry. Carefully pull the lettuce apart and fill each leaf with the lovage, apple, and carrot mixture. Garnish with onion rings and serve as a starter.

Sorrel, Rumex scutatus

This is not the large-leafed variety which can be found growing wild on sunny banks and in meadows but the French or Spanish sorrel, _Rumex scutatus_, which can be eaten for refreshment if you are thirsty. Select a sound whole leaf, preferably young and therefore light green. It can also be added to salads according to taste – mine is with Iceberg lettuce or endive. Chop lettuce and sorrel into fine strips and then dress with pepper, salt, oil, vinegar, and some sugar – preferably cane sugar.

Sorrel soup

Melt 50g (2oz) of butter in a pan and add to it 50g (2oz) of finely chopped sorrel. Allow to simmer gently until the sorrel is soft. Then add one litre (2pt) of water and 250g (8oz) of sliced potatoes. Season to taste with salt and pepper and let it simmer for an hour. Sieve the

In wet areas, herbs are best planted in slightly raised beds to keep excessive water from them. Place grey sage, cotton lavender (Santolina chamaecyparissus), and thyme together with green Galium (synonymous with Asperula) and rue for decoration and usefulness.

soup or mix in a blender. Beat the yolk of an egg, then add some of the soup to the egg and mix well. Pour into the remainder of the soup, reheat and serve.

Lemon balm in partial-shade

Melissa officinalis is the name for this bushy plant, which is extremely hardy. The flowers are white and they really attract bees. Lemon balm can be used to make tea and a few leaves can be added to soup.

A delicious dessert from lemon balm is made as follows. Peel two large oranges and chop or slice the peel finely. Remove the pith from the oranges and separate the segments. Sprinkle the lemon balm onto the oranges. If desired two teaspoons of Cointreau can be added. Put half a cup of cane sugar and the same amount of water into a pan and allow the sugar to melt over gentle heat. Pour half of this mixture over the orange segments and allow to cool. Put the orange peel in the remaining half of the melted sugar and water mixture and cook for ten minutes. Then allow to cool. Serve the segments of orange with ice- cream or creme fraiche and some of the sauce from the cooked peel. This is also delicious served hot.

Lemon balm as cure against loss of memory

Take 60g (2oz) of lemon balm and pour 1 litre (2pt) of boiling water over it. Allow this to steep for no longer than twenty minutes. The drink is then ready. Add sugar, honey, or lemon juice to taste. It is

This garden which I designed has vegetables and herbs close to the house. The herb beds can be seen and also behind the terrace there are currant bushes grown as standards.

Left: This miniature herb garden is just sufficient to grow some chives, mint and lemon balm in pots which are set in the soil. Thyme grows in pots on the balustrade.

believed to help people avoid loss of memory and generally keep their wits about them. If so, it is something to drink regularly!

Comfrey   Comfrey or *Symphytum officinale* will survive in partial shade, and there are varieties which are happy as ground-cover plants in places where there is a little shade.

Comfrey is commonly found in the wild, and it has pretty flowers with purple, white, or red bells. These colours and a number of variations are all often found. Comfrey tea is good for throat ailments and for colds. Pick 60g (2oz) of leaves and pour 1 litre (2pt) of boiling water over them. Allow to steep for half an hour and drink with honey; this is ideal for sore throats. The leaves can be filled with apple turnover mixture, dipped in batter, and fried as fritters. Serve with icing sugar. This herb is happy in partial shade, which is the bane of many town gardens – where there are trees and walls, inevitably there is shade. Yet shade undoubtedly offers exciting possibilities for gardeners who enjoy cooking.

Those who want to make a bouquet of flowers will need large-leafed foliage. For the base of the bouquet, Hosta is perfect; it lasts for some time and the plant is a jewel in the garden.

Children in the garden

A perfect lawn, fantastic border, and faultless rose garden are ambitions for the grown-ups to strive for and to enjoy. For children though it is a pain constantly to hear "look out", "stop playing football", and "go and play in the street..."

The children-friendly garden need not be a jumble of discarded toys or an excuse for the parents to do absolutely nothing with it "because of the children." When I was a child there were lots of places to play. Not on the front lawn, though; that was far too much on show. The back garden was fine for table tennis on the lawn, reading a book on one's stomach, or playing in the wooden summer-house with a cupboard full of secretive bits of rope, trowels, rakes, and shears. There, my brothers and sister played school or doctors and nurses for ever (my father was a doctor so there were ample but awesome discarded blunt scissors and plenty of bandages). Later my own children's garden was situated under a lilac which I saved from destruction. I bought it for next to nothing. Beneath it was planted *Ajuga*, bedstraw (or *Galium,* synonymous with *Asperula*), sedge from the wild, Solomon's seal, and my first box hedge, grown from cuttings. All of this was out of sight of the decorative garden which could be seen from the street and from the terrace near the house. It is not such a bad idea to divide the garden into a part to be on show, a nursery to raise plants, and an area for the children which can be claimed back and added to the rest of the garden when the children are older. Such a children's garden does not need masses of space. It can be a couple of beds surrounded by a box hedge or a piece of ground next to a sand-pit. Not every child will react positively to the offer to create such a special garden for them – one of my own did not.

Gateways, walls, hedges, and secretive groves permit surprise and another dimension. Such an attractive feature can provide the basic inspiration for a garden's design.

A way to make them enthusiastic is to give them sunflower seeds and introduce an element of competition that includes yourself. If you plant lettuce, let them have some for their garden. They are given *Cosmos* 'Bright Lights Series', the adults get chervil; the children harvest radishes, the parents pick a bunch from an old-time rose.

An integrated front garden

Sometimes people want everything, especially in towns, but it is just not possible. House hunters may have visited many houses when suddenly there is a house with the right number of rooms, a good position in the right neighbourhood but a rather small garden. Sometimes people continue to look, without realizing the possibilities of the small garden. This came home to me through designing a garden for a young couple with two children. The father was always busy and the mother was determined to return to work. Grandparents and children all had their own wishes. The front garden had only one advantage, a tall round holly hedge so dense that no passing cars or people could be seen. The only other notable features were an area of grass divided by a straight path to the front door at the side of the house, and a terrace near the living room at a higher level than the rest of the garden.

The idea of giving the children their own patch of garden which would be an integral part of the overall garden occurred when the pergola with a swing came into the picture. The pergola was to run above the

Children will spend hours in rapt wonderment by a pond in their own garden, studying the marvellous life that unfolds before them.

*Wires have been
stretched across the
rim of the pond to
discourage herons*

lengthened path to the front door, over beds with perennials, several hedges, and lots of grass. To create the maximum illusion of space, artificial turf that blended well with real grass was laid under the swing. The path to the front door is veiled with hedges so that visitors to the front door no longer see the entire garden from the gate. The roses and perennials were planted in raised beds because there were so many tree roots in the ground that new plants would barely have stood a chance. Taking everything into account, there was quite an investment in that garden, with new paths for children's games and to protect the grass from footsteps when wet. Hedges large and small created plenty of corners where children could do their own gardening without disturbing the effect of the decorative garden.

**Give children a
sunny spot**

Sometimes one sees children's gardens hidden away in some dark shady corner. That is neither fair nor very encouraging. Children are always likely to lack confidence in the garden if their parents are fanatical gardeners, who mow lawns, dig gardens, spray and water plants, prick out seedlings, and all those other garden tasks. A lack of confidence will be made worse by plants failing to grow through being in a bad spot, or poor soil, or because of too little sunlight or no protection from the wind.

My advice is to create a patch for each child and for yourself, marked out with box. This can become the experimental vegetable, cut-flower, or herb garden which can be filled with other plants later when the children leave home, if not earlier.

**A slice of pie for
adventure**

An old yet still good way to create a garden divided into areas is to make a circle with pie-slice segments. This idea is used extensively with roses, herbs, and vegetables. Recently I made a star-shaped garden with shells at its centre and alongside the paths.

Give each child a slice of pie and fill the remainder with vegetables and herbs. Later this can be turned into a beautiful herb garden or a combination with roses. It is important to define the shape clearly by planting a box hedge or one of lavender, or by laying a circular path to surround it – provided it is clearly defined. Fill the segments with plants which are not too tall such as thyme, hyssop, and lavender. For taller features use standards such as *Rosa* 'Iceberg' with its endless flowers, or red currants and blackcurrants for bountiful crops.

*Cultivation beds
alongside the
flower garden*

Not all town gardens are small. I found this out when asked to alter an already landscaped garden. Sometimes I can be very rigorous. On this occasion I proposed changing the character of the garden from a countryside look to a formal style. In small gardens and even medium-sized ones, the attempt to give an illusion of space through a countryside approach can go wrong.

This was proved for me by a garden than had a summer-house cum shed that was at least 1.8m (6ft) higher than the level of the house. The lawn sloped gently upwards from the house to the shed, which was easily accessible. My hatred of sloping lawns, at least those of small dimensions, resulted in a level lawn near the house and a steep slope as one approached the much higher shed. On either side of the lawn there were almost identical borders with roses and perennials, and in the space left over from this symmetrical design a vegetable garden was introduced to the right as one looked from the house. In addition there was room for box hedges, topiary chickens, and peacocks in box; and among all these there was also space for a children's garden.

These strong purple colours can be anticipated, with Phlox paniculata-hybride 'Aida', with honesty and with purple varieties of Hesperis.

Let the children choose their own spot

It is not always easy to get children interested in gardening. Fortunately there are often school gardens where the class works together on a small plot. Children often want to get into everything, playing games with other children or exercising on the swings but gardening is perhaps something their parents want them to do. To get them involved in the whole garden, it can be a good idea to let them choose their own patch of ground, so that they do not feel pressured – since that leads to a dampening of any enthusiasm. There are two ways for parents to set about it. You can give your children complete freedom to choose where they would like to have their garden, which will inevitably lead to it being placed slap in the middle of your

Peacocks strut like divas. Of course, their wretched shrieks will never win over an audience such as one at La Scala in Milan.

intended terrace. That's where the sunflowers will grow which give them so much pleasure, where the sickly looking leeks will be, and also the mass of orange African marigolds. Or you can let them select from a choice of sites which suit you, yet which can be seen from their bedroom or their place at the table, or are close to the terrace. Children want constantly to check what is happening. Of course the second way is better: you give them a number of choices and the result is their garden, enclosed or not.

Wood pigeons are wild birds, free in the woods. For those who wish to see doves or pigeons close to the house a dovecote is a possibility.

When I was young apparently I become more and more enthusiastic. Plants costing nothing came from everywhere and were collected from the woods or grass verges. Spare plants to be planted in my own garden came from the main flower garden in exchange for helping my parents. I cannot remember if I ever bought any plants. Yellow flag came from a ditch to form part of the permanent planting. It did tremendously well, even underneath trees and without a pond in sight. Mint also came from the edge of the ditch along with meadowsweet, which was also planted in a none too-sunny position. Sometimes I was given plants. My older neighbours will never be forgotten because of the cigar box full of creeping *Ajuga* and bedstraw they gave me for my little garden. That grown-ups valued what I did with my garden was an enormous boost. My fanatical gardening parents let me gradually take over more and more of the garden without any difficulties arising between us. Eventually I started to involve myself with the main flower garden, the cut flowers, and suchlike. It resulted in my deciding to become a gardener. That is the best basis for a landscape architect. My interest in plants was awakened, not stifled, by my parents.

Deadly for enthusiasm: having to cut the grass

Many garden owners tell me how as children they were made to cut the grass every Saturday afternoon, resulting in their present hatred of the garden. That is quite understandable. Tell the children that the entire family is responsible for the home and garden. Clearly in some families that was not the understanding, or perhaps it was understood but ignored, resulting in a life-long hatred of gardening for some.

Yet once someone gets their own piece of land, such as the small piece of ground behind a brand new house, then with parents no longer breathing down their necks their interest returns by fits and starts. When there is a self-choice of what is planted and pride from the results, early enthusiasm may return. Garden owners for whom weekly grass cutting worked the wrong way, however well intentioned as an upbringing, may regain a love of the garden. Hopefully this will have the result of a lovely children's garden for their offspring in a sunny spot – not hidden away – with well-fed soil where they can choose what to grow.

A delightful outside dining area was created in this garden on a large terrace with brick pavers. White-flowering perennials, roses, and busy lizzies display themselves in a pot.

Ponds fascinate children

Some time ago I unexpectedly visited a large garden in a centuries-old town with a medieval centre. There was lots of grass and also winding paths with shrubs and perennials and a pond.

The children who constantly sat around the pond during my stay or ran around it with shrimping nets were between three and four years old. They studied insects on the water, the little fish in it, and the dragon-flies which flew over their heads. In short, they were absorbed by the waterside.

This experience convinced me that children cannot be denied a pond. The difficulties are well known. Children not yet able to swim are in great danger of drowning. Yet there are ways of having both a pond and children together in the garden.

Railings around the pond: a temporary measure

A pond can be built at any time. During construction, bear in mind that if there are children in the family who cannot swim, dark green metal railings or a green plasticized mesh can be used to surround the pool. Children will thereby be prevented from falling in. Such a fence need not be high: 50cm (20in) is sufficient. Low metal railings like the ones seen in parks look fine. The rails should be as thin as possible and project some way above the top horizontal bar through which or against which they are welded. With railings 50cm (20in) high above ground, the rails can project 20cm (8in) above the bar. The distance between top and bottom bar would be 30cm (12in).

A fence of green plasticized mesh

Choose thin aluminium poles of moss green aluminium, plastic, or steel and mesh of the same colour. Those wanting a simple, cheap solution for what is to be a temporary fence can use round wooden poles about 70 to 80cm long (28 to 32in), driven 30 to 40cm (12 to 16in) into the ground, leaving about 50cm (20in) sticking above ground. Paint or stain the poles green or dark green to match the mesh and fix the mesh with a wire or with fencing staples. The latter have the advantage that children cannot remove them, in spite of their interest in finding out how things are constructed.

Mesh in the pond

Obtain a large reinforcing mesh for concrete, cut to the internal dimensions of the pond by the supplier. Place piles of small slabs on the bottom of the pond so that they come to about 10 to 15cm (4 to 6in) under the surface. Place the reinforcing mesh on the piles of slabs. The child who falls in will fall onto the mesh. Fine green mesh can be placed on top to prevent any risk of children's feet falling through the gaps. To make a really thorough job, paint the mesh black so that it is not noticeable. You should do this in the winter or just after the installation of the pond, before the bog and water plants start to grow, so that you avoid disturbing them. Water-lilies will grow through the mesh, soon making it invisible.

Sometimes, when you have done enough gardening or are tired after a long journey, you just want to be among plants, listening to birds; do so lazing in a garden chair.

Play equipment in the town garden

Children like cheerful colours, according to parents. Yet a study of what children make for themselves reveals greyish bits of timber used to make little huts and bridges. Whoever thought up the idea that children like bright colours for their play equipment should be banished to Disneyland.

My experience is that children like natural materials that seem old. In my own gardens, gaudy climbing frames and swings have quickly disappeared. Of course, children are sometimes so attached to brightly painted equipment that it should be allowed to remain, whether you get away with painting over it in green or not.

Fortunately there are many alternative timber colours, and wood weathers to grey or can be stained with dark wood shades for swings, climbing frames, and little dens.

From swing to pergola

Where possible, I try to fix a swing and climbing rope to a solidly constructed pergola. Of course, the pergola has to be well built of good materials, perhaps with extra supports at the bottom of the uprights to hold it firm. These can later be removed.

Another option is to concrete the foot of the upright and fix everything with good bolts, because two children in full swing can exert a

Here a sand-pit (right) and a chicken run have been built next to each other in a garden.

Next page: Wooden decking could make an attractive feature for almost every garden. Bear in mind that timber becomes slippery when wet after a heavy shower of rain.

53

lot of force on the structure. Let grapes grow over the pergola; children will find those fascinating and they will enjoy certainly eating the ripe fruit.

The aim is to integrate the pergola into the whole garden plan so that when the children grow out of playing on the swing, the initial outlay can be put to use for the benefit of the entire garden.

From sand-pit to pond or herb garden

A sand-pit can be portable so that it can be moved to be near the place where you sit – small children feel happiest close to their parents – or you can site it permanently where it suits you. This means that if the sand-pit is on view in an attractive part of the garden, it needs to be made pleasant to look at. So no more large red plastic tubs surrounded by sand with clashing coloured toys, but something nicer instead. Try to make a rim to sit on, where sand pies can be "baked", and if possible choose wood as the edging of the sand-pit. Sleepers are cheap but often none too clean, unless older ones are available. Build walls to a depth of 50cm (20in) below ground level because energetic children will dig at least that deep in this play place dedicated to them. A sand-pit is therefore actually a hole in the ground with slabs at its bottom and timber walls of 70cm (28in) or so, with 20cm (8in) sticking out above the ground providing somewhere to sit. When it is finished, fill the pit with clean sand (river sand is best if available) and

Creating different areas in a garden provides places for hidden enjoyment for child and adult alike. Avoid the open garden in which everything is on view.

Left: There are garden features which animals are mad about, such as rose hips for birds. Dry paving is for dogs. They do not like wet grass. Tables and chairs are just the thing for cats to sun themselves in the dry.

cover it against stray cats and dogs which will otherwise find it a first-class toilet. The easiest way is to make a frame to fit and cover it with wire netting. No dog or cat will sit on this. A complete lid is possible, preferably fixed with a hinge so it can be lifted and hooked back to stop it unexpectedly falling down. With a complete lid, the sand will remain dry even in endlessly wet winters. Since I have never played in a sand-pit, even as a child, I am passing on what I have heard from parents. Quite why a child should not play in wet sand is beyond me since I should think wet sand is much more suitable to dig in and to mould, but I understand dry sand is what they want. It makes me melancholy to recall the beaches and dunes that were my own gigantic sand-pit. The ground was wet more often than it was dry, and it was never boring.

The sand-pit can later be turned into a pond; the wooden-walled pit can be utilized and the sand can act as a foundation for paving or a patio. Another option is to remove the sand and replace it with soil. Then with little extra work or cost the ideal herb garden can be made. The timber wall will prevent even the most rampant plants such as mint from taking over the entire garden.

Children in the garden
The small town garden in the diagram is broken up into different sections with thought given to the paved areas. There is a sun terrace

Statues used to be constrained by formal settings and patterns. Give them freedom among the plants for a more romantic garden, avoiding formality.

and a shady terrace. Shadow is created by a *Prunus cerasifera*, the red-leafed *Prunus* (sited at 5), which blooms early in spring. The roses and perennials are therefore restricted to purple, pink, and soft blue. A low wall to sit on is a nice place for children to enjoy a tray of drinks and snacks. The sand-pit is also here and can be converted into a pond later.

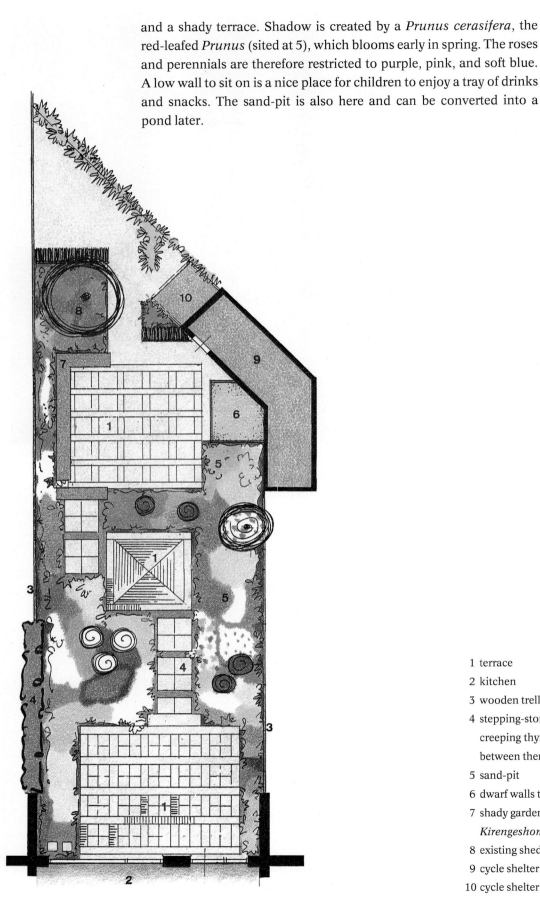

1 terrace

2 kitchen

3 wooden trellis with grapes

4 stepping-stones of existing slabs with creeping thyme, *Thymus languginosus*, between them

5 sand-pit

6 dwarf walls to sit on

7 shady garden with *Hosta* and *Kirengeshoma palmata*

8 existing shed

9 cycle shelter

10 cycle shelter

Precious and sturdy roses

For many, a garden cannot exist without roses. No doubt they are right to follow their own preference, but there are town gardens in which I would never dare to plant a single one. Those that insist on roses in unsuitable places are simply egoistic.

Rose macrantha *'Raubritter' has round, pink pom-pom blooms. It can also be used as a climber.*

Fortunately there are roses which even under such inappropriate circumstances will give a display of blooms. A climbing rose such as *Rosa* 'Zepherine Drouhin', the thornless violet rose which has a wonderful scent, is able to tolerate positions with no sun and still flower. The same rose placed in the sun would probably be more vigorous and would climb higher. Another which will definitely flower in a sunless spot provided there is plenty of light is *Rosa* 'New Dawn' which produces really long tendrils. It is a sturdy rose, perhaps the sturdiest there is with the exception of the really too brightly coloured *Rosa* 'Paul's Scarlet.' This deep red rose is truly able to withstand almost anything the cruellest gardener could think of. Poor soil, wind, drought, wet, shade, it can cope with them all, although it is possible to tell it is not doing so well by changed leaf colour, reduced growth, and less abundant flowering.

Besides climbing roses, there are floribunda or cluster roses that are almost indestructible and flower year after year in even a totally neglected garden. There is a lesson here. Choose the strongest roses for a new garden since the conditions in the town garden are more often unfavourable than favourable. This is because shrubs and trees grow and the area of shade gets larger. The ground is also rapidly depleted of nutrients and becomes sour and poorly aerated – not really the right soil for roses. Yet if we truly want roses, we can change all this and find out what their needs are.

The best circumstances for roses in the town garden

Let's begin with the ideal situation: a sunny garden with rich soil; no large trees; no hedges, walls, house facade, or shrubs to create shade; and conditions that are neither too dry nor too damp. Remarkably, roses like rich heavy soil and do as wonderfully well on clay as on a good loam or alluvium. In summer when the ground is baked hard they send their roots down into deeper regions. They do not like soil which remains wet well into spring and drainage is therefore necessary in such circumstances so that the roots can stay dry, safely above the water table. This has been proved by the Dutch rose growers Moerheim. They had a monopoly on new roses from the French rose growers Meilland.

Creating new varieties of roses

In Antibes, a pretty old town situated on a peninsula between Nice and Cannes, there are right at the tip rose growers known as Meilland who have been going for generations. In their greenhouses, which I have visited several times, roses are grown from seed with the intention of finding new varieties to cultivate for the commercial and private market. The nursery divides roses into two types, those for displays in the garden and those for growing in greenhouses to provide cut flowers. The method of finding new varieties is the same for both. The first thing is to discover what new properties people want in a rose, a yellower tint, more red, more pink, white blooms, and so on. Often the starting point is known healthy roses that flower well. The search is perhaps for a different colour or more colours, or greater height or a more attractive leaf. Crossing roses is known as hybridizing. Pollen from, for example a yellow rose, is introduced to the pistil of a pure white rose. The resulting seed which is subsequently removed from the rose hip is sown in one of the long greenhouses at the Meilland rose growers. Then comes the waiting, waiting for the seed to germinate, another year's wait for the plant to flower. I visited once in May when the houses were full of roses blooming, thousands of them from which the rose growers must make a choice. Careful consideration is given to the quality of the blooms and the length of flowering, to the leaves, and resistance to disease. If a rose survives the first selection then it is grafted on to a root stock. The root stock generates stronger, more disease resistant growth – at least, it usually does. The rose is then moved outdoors to study its reaction to sun, rain, cold, and drought.

A straight path leads to the back of the garden. It sounds rather rigid but the reality is a romantically planted town garden with flagstones.

If this is all fine, then the rose is submitted to the international registration authority for roses, which judges roses from different growers. Each year a selection is made by the international rose experts and only when they grant a certificate to a rose may it be brought onto the market.

The Moerheim rose growers had the monopoly on the sale of Meilland roses for both the garden and the commercial greenhouse. When these roses were planted out in the trial grounds they did not seem to thrive. The trial grounds were in rather damp fenland and

the soil did not warm up quickly. The roses cultivated in France – used to sun, drought, and mild winters – could not cope with their new conditions and they suffered. These roses did much better on sandy soils or on clay. There are still roses from Moerheim's range which are widely used, such as the irreplaceable *Rosa* 'Swaney', whose white clusters are long lasting. It is no ground-cover rose, but the stems, which hang delightfully over dwarf walls, do not grow longer than 50cm (20in). Roses grown in northern Europe tend to do better in the harsher climate, as do species and old garden roses. These are easy roses to grow in the town garden, with just one abundant flowering per season.

The strongest white cluster-flowered rose is Rosa *'Iceberg', which flowers here together with lady's mantle.*

Species and old garden roses

There are various types of these roses. Firstly let us consider gallica roses. These originate from the area of Europe given this name by the Romans, which is more or less equivalent to modern day France. The gallica roses actually originate from central and southern Europe and are true shrub roses which send out underground runners so that they become an ever greater mass. The way to cultivate them is by division. Take a part of the plant, complete with root, and plant it elsewhere. Generally the height of them is about 1m (3ft). 'Cardinal de Richelieu' becomes 1.5 to 2m tall (3 to 6ft) and has a double flower of deep purple, essential for romantics who adore strong colours and intense emotions. 'Charles de Mills' has the

61

L'Hay des Roses.

largest flower of them all, more violet-purple in colour. 'Duchess d'Angloueme' is as delicate as a butterfly-like young duchess with delicate pink outer petals to match her cheeks and a warmer centre. 'Duchesse de Montebello' does not have fiery Italian colouring but is delicate and can grow 2m (6ft) tall. 'Empress Josephine' is named for the first wife of Napoleon; she cultivated many roses at Malmaison. The collection of her roses has been kept intact in the living rose museum of L'Hay des Roses at Anthony, a southern suburb of Paris. The colour of the rose bearing her name is magenta with somewhat darker veins. It remains low growing. *Rosa gallica* 'Officinalis' also remains a low shrub, displaying semi-double blush crimson flowers with yellow stamens. This is the oldest gallica rose and it quickly spreads. After flowering, growth is concentrated in the lower stems, which is far better, as otherwise the garden becomes a mess.

Also known as 'The Apothecary's Rose', the 'Officinalis' is grown for its petals which are pressed for perfume, its rose oil that is used in the kitchen in all manner of drinks, and rose hips that are used as a herb and by serious cooks. *Rosa gallica* 'Versicolour' (*Rosa* 'Mundi') is from the 'Officinalis' species and has long been known for its petals that have light lilac to crimson striping on a pale blush-pink background. It grows no taller than 1.5m (5ft). 'Tuscany' is one of the deepest coloured gallica roses, in deep blue, almost velvety

The pergola is so decorative that the roses seem to be almost unnecessary additions. Rosa 'Buff Beauty' is flowering here.

purple with yellow stamens. The 'Tuscany Superb' is a shrub rose which grows somewhat larger and has bigger flowers. It will have been a seedling from the parent 'Tuscany' which an attentive grower once saved and cultivated. This is how many gallica roses came about. Enthusiasts and growers introduced the pollen from a darker coloured flower to a lighter one, sowed the seed from the hips which appear in the autumn, and obtained a new variety, which is just slightly different than its parents.

A pleasantly inspiring use

At the castle of Walenburg in the Netherlands there is a good example of how gallica roses can be used. There are two islands of which one is a rose garden, more of which later.

On the south side of the private island shrubs have been planted which have grown into trees. There is *Gleditsia triacanthos* 'Inermis' and a winter-flowering *Prunus subhirtella* 'Autumnalis' which provide shade, together with centuries-old oak trees on the other side of the moat. Yet gallica roses thrive here as a semi-circular hedge surrounding a place to sit. They encircle a stone table with stone seats. In spite of being in partial shade, the roses grow into a cheerful hedge that flowers adequately, though less abundantly than in full sun.

The stems of *Rosa gallica* 'Versicolour', otherwise known as 'Rosa Mundi' (this is the same rose, with – very confusingly – two different

For those who want to assemble a large collection of shrub roses, a large garden will be necessary unless the roses are placed close to each other and trained upwards on supports. Here at Castle Walenburg in the Netherlands, which has open days for the public, metal reinforcing bars have been used as sticks. They rust slightly and are indestructible and cheap.

63

names, each given long ago), bend easily so they need tying to supports. At Walenburg the roses are all tied to stakes of rusting concrete reinforcing bars, which have an almost endless life. They do not stand out between the shrubs which form almost a hedge, each shrub being linked to the next by steel wire which also rusts and winds its way through the branches. By using two wires, all the branches are held firm. New shoots are either fixed to the wire or pushed between the wires. For a romantic place to sit in the garden, plant gallica roses around the spot chosen, preferably ones of the same type. Their care-free growth ensures there will be no stiff formality.

Damask roses In the fourteenth century roses were probably taken by returning crusaders – to, for instance, France, where Robert de Brie planted them at his castle. From there they have spread forth.

My favourites include 'Celsiana' with its large clear pure pink flowers and golden-yellow stamens. This is an exquisitely fragrant rose, which grows 1.5m (5ft) high.

'Madame Hardy' has white flowers which are initially slightly pink and produce a delightful scent. It was named by the gardener of Josephine de Beauharnais for his wife. 'Quatre Saisons' becomes a broad bushy shrub with grey-green leaves and clear pink flowers, reaching 1.5m (5ft) high.

Trelliswork can be quite simple. Fix battens horizontally and vertically. If hardwood is used it will last for ages.

Rosa damascena 'Versicolour' is also known as the 'York and Lancaster' rose. I have specifically used the Latin name because there is also, as we saw earlier, a 'Versicolour' *Rosa gallica*. These two roses look like each other, with crimson to violet stripes on petals of white to pale blush-pink.

Alba roses Alba roses resulted from crossing the dog rose and other wild roses and they tolerate partial shade. The dog rose Rosa *canina* is widely distributed in the wild throughout Europe and was crossed long ago by nature itself. They are of the larger variety of roses, reaching a considerable height, and they bear flowers with tints from pure white through to plain pink. The flowers are always lovely and delicate and they bring something refined to the indestructible spinney or grove. *Rosa alba-maxima* is often known as 'Great Double White' and also as the 'Jacobite rose.' When this white rose came into existence is unknown, but it is well recognized as one of the strongest shrub roses there is, and that means almost indestructible. *Rosa alba semi-plena* grows lushly and has greyish foliage. The flowers are white and are succeeded by delightful hips. This 'Rose of York' is a must for the decorative garden, not just because of its exuberant flowering but also for its height of 2m (6ft) which make it look dramatic between hollies, lilacs, and magnolias. 'Bel Amour' has salmon-pink flowers which means it is a good acquisition for

Rosa *'Bonica' is the mauve one,* Rosa *'The Fairy' is the smallest, and* Rosa *'Betty Prior' is the tallest of the roses in this border in Salisbury, England. The choice in this range of colours is considerable.*

65

many. The scent is spicy, some say like myrrh, explaining why it was previously planted in cloisters. The flowers were probably used in incense holders. 'Celestial' has double flowers tinted a soft pink, broken by yellow stamens. It was discovered in the Dutch province of Holland in the nineteenth century. 'Felicite Parmentier' is a much-loved rose, which will, however, only appreciate rich soil. 'Madame Plantier' has pompom-like cream flowers. It is a large rose, which can be trained as a climber. 'Great Maiden's Blush' has a light pink tint which lightens slightly at the tips of the petals. A more delightful name is 'Cuisse de Nymphe Emue' or thigh of a passionate nymph, conjuring up notions of light pink which is precisely the colour of this very old variety, which was already planted in sixteenth-century gardens. 'Konigin von Danemarck', otherwise known as 'Belle Courtisanne', is a warm pink rose, famous for its perfect urn-shaped flowers. The flowers are quartered, the foliage is grey-green, and the bush remains fairly low at about lm (3ft). The flower is much beloved and very elegant.

This old garden has a formal layout in which the grass acts as a resting point for the eye and gives a focus to the centrepiece.

Provence or centifolia roses

These are the flowers which almost always featured in still-life paintings of the eighteenth and nineteenth centuries, with their large double flowers, hanging decoratively in clusters. The flowers are so heavy that head-up, facing towards the sky blooms cannot generally be expected. Fortunately the growth of these roses is so strong that

they can be viewed from below, at the side of the bush. Occasionally the weight of the flowers is not so much of a problem and orderly flowers can be seen standing up, provided the bush is low. The colours are mainly white-pink.

Rosa centifolia has many local names, used in areas where they are to be found in many gardens. The name 'Provence Rose' is used by the many artists who painted it time after time, from which comes one alternative name, 'Rose des Peintres.' The flowers are large, hanging and beautiful. They grow taller than 1.5m (5ft). This is an old rose which probably resulted from crossing with other even older roses. It was known as early as 1600.

'Chapeau de Napoleon' should perhaps be planted alongside *Rosa* 'Empress Josephine' and *Rosa* 'Madame Hardy.' Add to them 'Souvenir de Malmaison' and we have created a Napoleonic revival. 'Chapeau de Napoleon' has a large cupped flower in attractive triangular form, rather like the emperor's famous tricorn hat. The colour is a delicate shade of pink. The rose is also known as the 'Crested Rose.' *Rosa* 'De Meaux' remains low growing and is therefore suitable for the edge of borders, as is 'Petite de Holland'. The colour of the many small roses is pink, their size about 2cm (3/4in) and their form usually pompom. This miniature bush rose was first cultivated in 1789. One of my favourite French painters is Henri Fantin Latour, who could capture the delicacy of roses and lilac like no

Rosa filipes *and* Rosa multiflora *have white flowers and they grow to tall shrubs or can be trained.*

Left: In the Parisian suburb of Anthony is L'Hay des Roses. Behind the arches of roses in the foreground can be seen a rectangular gateway with metal latticework festooned with white double roses of an old variety. Nameplates are placed throughout the garden to help visitors make their own selection of historical roses.

other. The rose named after him eventually becomes a broad bush bearing flowers with a delicate blush which smell fantastic. Its height is up to 1.5m (5ft). On a different scale is 'Petite de Holland', which is planted in my own Dutch garden in Zeeland clay and grows to 50cm (20in) with pink flowers of tiny form. This rose looks good at the front of a border. 'De Bischop' (The Bishop) has crimson red flowers which appear light violet on the underside of the petals. With its depth of colour, this rose comes close to being a blue rose. 'Tour de Malakoff' is magenta appearing violet later. The eye-catching large blooms are double flower rosettes with a height of 1.8m (6ft).

Moss roses, renowned for their buds

In the main it is the centifolia roses that become clothed around the buds with what resembles moss in significant amounts. Moss roses were known as early as the eighteenth century in France and by 1850, when they had been hybridized and cultivated on a large scale, they had become popular.

'Comtesse de Murinais' has white flowers, although the bud which is surrounded by dark green moss is pink. It grows to 1.8m (6ft). 'Duchesse de Verneuil' has a refined appearance and pure pink flowers, growing to more than lm (3ft) if kept free from disease.

'General Kleber' must have been a man of gentle disposition, judging by the delicate pink rose with a green fleck at its centre that bears his name. The bush stays fairly low, making it an excellent choice for informal hedging, with the mossy buds providing extra beauty. It has an attractive scent too. 'Gloire de Mousseaux' has extremely large flowers, perhaps the largest of all the old roses. It grows to 1.8m (6ft) and has soft pink flowers. 'Henri Martin', also known as 'Red Moss' has purplish-red double-flowered rosettes with only a little moss. A major plus of 'Henri Martin' is the many rose hips which this 1.8m (6ft) shrub bears.

Stone used to be worked to make gutters and drinking troughs. Such antique features make delightful bird baths if the drainage holes are bunged up.

'Mousseline or 'Alfred de Dalmas' is planted particularly for its second flowering, for there are two chances to enjoy its cupped double flowers of blush pink. It is perfect for low hedges with its delightful flowers and a height of 1.2m (4ft).

'Nuits de Young' is almost black, hence its other name 'Old Black', with dark maroon-purple flowers lightened by yellow stamens. The dark green leaves are also interesting because of the somewhat purplish tinge they reflect. Its growth is rather limited 'Shailer's White Moss' is the best white moss rose and grows to 1.2m (4ft).

'William Lobb', also known as 'Duchesse d'Istrie', is often planted for its height, some 2m (6ft). It has a cheerful magenta colour. It always bears many flowers in clusters. Each flower is double, in rosette form, and each has lots of moss on the underside. An extra feature of this rose is that it will also climb when trained to an arch or through other shrubs.

China roses These roses have the characteristic of continued flowering, which is not the case with all old roses. Roses are found in China in the wild, just as they are in many countries of the northern hemisphere. Chinese wild roses had the advantage of continued flowering, unlike European wild roses, and so the crossing of the Chinese ones with European roses opened up major new developments in rose growing.

Some of the roses that were once imported to Europe are still available and are highly appreciated. 'Hermosa' is an elegant bush with fairly small, fine cupped light pink flowers to be enjoyed all summer long. *Rosa mutabilis* is an open grower, with elegant purple-violet flowers which are light pink on the inside. There is no great profusion of flowers and this bush is suitable for placing in a border with perennials, on its own, or as a group weaving through the other plants. 'Old Blush' is an open rose which starts its continuous flowering at the end of May. The bush grows 1m (3ft) high. The scent is refined and remarkably similar to that of the sweet pea. The colour is a soft pink.

'Sophie's Perpetual' has dark red flowers on a 2m (6ft) high shrub. It is often used as a climber. 'Viridiflora' bears green roses which are beautiful in the green-soft yellow-white garden and a must for collectors and flower arrangers. It stays as a low shrub. It begins flowering in June, and it continues flowering throughout the summer.

Shrub roses have been trained upwards so that the rich flowering can be seen above the perennials.

Portland roses   These roses were especially popular in the eighteenth century, when their strong magenta colour was highly regarded.

'Comte de Chambord', or 'Madame Knorr' as it is otherwise known, has quartered pink fully double rosette flowers of 10cm (4in) across on a bush growing to 1.5m (5ft). 'Indigo' has deep purple flowers on a 1m (3ft) high bush. 'Jacques Cartier' has large clear pink flowers with a green centre. This rose too has a warm pink colour and grows no taller than 1m (3ft). The flower is fully double. 'The Portland' is a wide bush with open roses which have star-like subtle yellow stamens. The flower is deep violet.

In the garden shown in Chapter 5 in which the fountain splashed from a wall, I designed this peaceful, classical pond. At each corner is a green topiary sphere.

Bourbon roses for a romantic garden   On the island of Mauritius in the Indian Ocean, the farmers always used to plant two sorts of rose intertwined together to form a hedge. These were 'Old Blush' and a number of varieties of the autumn damask rose. 'Old Blush' is a China rose with continued flowering, and the damask roses flower twice a year. Among all the roses on the island, hybrids have occurred, of which one was sent to the court of King Louis Philippe. This is how the name of the bourbon rose originated, since the French king was of the house of Bourbon. Remove the wilting flowers and feed the bush well with manure and the second flowering of these roses will be stunning.

'Boule de Neige' becomes 1.5m (5ft) high and bears crimson buds which open as creamy flowers sometimes tinged with pink. The

combination of white flowers with red-white buds is unique. 'Bourbon Queen' is sturdy and will survive periods of neglect, which is a good recommendation for a plant in the town garden. The bush is 1.5m (5ft) high and is easily trained. The flower is pink with darker pink veining. 'Coupe d'Hebe' is upright and suitable for growing against walls, pergolas, and summer-houses, where the thin growth is suitable. The flowers are pink cups. 'Honorine de Brabant' has lilac-pink double cupped flowers marked with light purple and crimson stripes. Its height is 1.8m (6ft) and it flowers a second time. Far taller at 2.5m (8ft) is 'Madame Isaac Pereire'. This has large leaves and blooms of at least 10cm (4in). 'Madame Pierre Oger' has creamy pink to rose-lilac tints, which are unusual. Do not plant it in a wet garden or the buds will go mouldy. It grows to 1.5m (5ft). 'Reine Victoria' is one of the most loved of bourbon roses and it is still planted in many gardens. It is 1.5m (5ft) high with rosette flowers in shades of pink to lilac-pink. 'Souvenir de Malmaison' fits in the Napoleonic corner, in the sun. This rose reaches lm (3ft) and bears a sea of cupped blooms which are later quartered rosettes.

'Souvenir de St Anne's' comes from a private garden in Dublin. It is 2m (6ft) high, bears delicate pink flowers and spreads a delightful strong scent. A rose discovered in Bologna, 'Variegata di Bologna', has everything for the rather decadent flower arranger; dark mauve stripes appear on the white petals, making the cupped flowers very

A path of grass leads one through delightful drifts of perennials at this farm. At the end is a statue.

attractive. They can be trained up to 3m (10ft) or grown as a bush of 1.8m (6ft). 'Zepherine Drouhin' is a deep pink climber with a strong colour and is thornless. It can also be grown as a bush.

Remontant roses: several continued flowering varieties

'Baronne A. de Rothschild' has large pink flowers, with a feast of a second flowering. It grows 1.2m (4ft) high. 'Baronne Prevost' also has soft pink flowers with the same height but somewhat flatter and clearly quartered flowers. They smell superb. 'Empereur de Maroe' is a velvet red. The flowers are fairly small and quartered. This rather weak bush is deliciously scented. 'Frau Karl Druschki' has another name, 'Reine des Neiges', which gives away its white colour. 'Paul Neyron' has the largest flower of this group of roses and is a delightful silver-pink. It remains a relatively low 1.5 to 1.8m (5 to 6ft), 'Reine des Violettes' or 'Queen of the Violets' has quartered rosette deep purple to violet flowers. 'Souvenir de Docteur Jamain' has deep crimson flowers and grows as a 1.5m (5ft) high bush. It is easily trained as the stems are rather soft.

Apart from these old roses there are of course more roses which are ideal for the garden. They are to be found in grower's catalogues and to be seen in many gardens. The previously named varieties are suited to the town garden and provide something of the romance necessary in such an enclosed garden. There are hybrid perpetual roses which continue flowering through summer and autumn, floribunda

To create atmosphere, place plants with apparent randomness so that blankets of colour are created. The effect is achieved here with the blue tint of Michaelmas daisies.

or cluster-flowered roses with several flowers per stem, and the famous roses of David Austin with which people are currently so infatuated – quite rightly. They have retained the period romance of the old roses whilst providing continued flowering. Everyone selling roses offers them in improbably beautiful colours. My intention will be achieved if, as the occupier of a town garden, you go hunting for the old, almost forgotten roses which have existed in town gardens for centuries. There are people who only collect women, roses with the lovely name of a woman, that is. Personally I prefer to have a theme based upon a century. I have already collected the seventeenth and eighteenth centuries and am now working on others. The best way to present roses, though, is to be strong-minded enough to stick to a colour scheme.

Roses in the town garden

Personally I do not like gardening solely with roses. The result is too much of the same, too many bushes similar in form, and too many flowers. Therefore I mix rose bushes with perennials, shrubs, and ground-cover plants. Always make sure there are evergreens because rose bushes look rather unattractive in winter unless species with attractive rose hips have been chosen. All species roses bear hips – such as *Rosa moyesii* synonymous with *Rosa* 'Geranium', which has bottle-shaped hips. The flowers are dusky scarlet and borne on attractive high arching stems.

In this garden full of grey foliage plants there are a number of varieties of shrub rose. The result is a magical misty ambience.

For those who want a white garden there is a wide choice. Mix different roses together to avoid a large area of one type; which would make a town garden too predictable. It is essential to try to maintain an element of surprise; hence mixing roses with other plants is an excellent idea. Perennials in shades of blue and white fit well with roses of all colours. There are also of course enough roses which bear solely white flowers. Combine upright plants in the background and on their own with lower, more spreading groups of violets, *Anaphalis,* or white Michaelmas daisies (*Aster cordifolius* 'Silver Spray'). Roses combine well with larkspur and yellow or cream roses with mullein (*Verbascum*). Round and vertical forms are fascinating, so that all pointed perennials such as *Polygonum amplexicaule* 'Roseum' are suitable, in this case with pink and purple roses. Grey foliage is important as a contrast to the green of the roses themselves and interesting leaf shapes provide variety. The delicate leaves of true *Geraniums* and varieties of *Dicentra* and varieties of *Dicentra eximia*, ferns, and *Euphorbia* also provide contrast. Choose also coarse-leafed foliage such as *Crambe cordifolia, Rheum tanguticum*, lady's mantle, with close leaf forms or the coarse round leaves of *Bergenia, Brunnera*, or the split leaves of *Anchusa, Cirsiuim, or Acanthus.*

Mixing roses with perennials

This chicken-peacock welcomes visitors to the garden at Hidcote Manor.

There are many cluster-flowered or floribunda roses which I constantly grow because of their sturdy nature and habit. *Rosa* 'Iceberg' is one of them, as are *Rosa* 'Little White Pet' and 'Marie Pavic.' The last two have the character of old roses and the small elegant form which is currently highly regarded for a romantic garden. Another strong rose, with a blush of rose in the cheeks of her white open petals, is 'Lady of the Dawn.'

'Maria Mathilda' has a pink bud but flowers on and on with white clusters of flowers. There are many delicate coloured cluster-flowering roses: 'Leersum 700' is a soft yellow, 'Amber Queen' is soft amber to subtle orange, 'Lilli Marleen' is amber-pink. Place them among abundant grey foliage, for that will make the bushes delicate, or with the low green foliage and white star clusters of the flowers of *Tiarella wherryi*. Place tall perennials here and there, such as the white mullein (*Verbascum*), white *Lysimachia ephemerum, Phlox*, and *Gaura*, which flowers all summer long.

These mixed borders are usually very successful, certainly where the shrub roses can be placed in the background they are. They flower maybe only once but that can be an advantage. The peaceful green shrubs act as a backdrop to the flowering plants in front. Creating a sense of calm is essential to avoid a chaotic, too busy result.

Inspiration from the rose garden of Castle Walenburg

This castle opens the gates of its gardens to visitors seven times each year during the different seasons so that people can see how in a relatively small area enormous variation can be achieved. There are

many parts of the garden, all separated from each other. There is a perennial garden, a peaceful garden with solely white flowering plants, a nursery garden with many roses for picking, and perennials in a greenhouse. There is a wild woodland garden in mini-format, and of course there is a rose garden.

However, roses are to be found everywhere. In the perennial borders they are used to provide tall areas of purple and pink. They climb amid the fruit trees in the peaceful garden. The section with long small borders is beautified with climbing roses which zoom out of the garden. They are trained over telegraph poles which are used as trestles, cut through the middle, and bolted together at the top, Over them grow roses such as 'Bobby James', with its conspicuously long stems.

In the cut-flower nursery there are solely dark red roses, specially planted for making bouquets. They are combined with larkspur, which is grown here in massive quantity.

The rose garden is surrounded on all sides by a hedge of *Carpinus betulus*, which is a light green and a perfect contrast to the lacklustre old shrub roses and bushes planted here. By old roses, I mean of course young plants of old roses. All the gallica, moss, alba, remontant, and damask roses referred to in this chapter are collected together in this garden. They are cut back each year to small bushes no higher than 1.5m (5ft) and they flower each year as a hedge on

Stachys byzantina *has felt-like grey leaves, hence the name bunnies' ears.*

Round tussocks of Hosta *and* Pennisetum, *the decorative grass, are used here to guide one through the plants placed along the path.*

the outer edge of the rose court. In the centre of the garden the roses are modern and perpetually flowering, therefore remontant. They are all chosen for their delicate colours. 'Dainty Bess' and 'Leersum 700' are next to the green *Rosa* 'Viridiflora.' There are ground-cover plants placed around the roses to maintain interest in spring and autumn and to avoid any formality or dullness.

Since the Dutch Garden Foundation appointed me to supervise these gardens, I have had many bulbs planted between the roses. Examples are soft pink lilies, anenomes, and *Allium* to make the spring into a feast of flowering. That has succeeded and from April the garden is a riot of blooms and a pleasure for the eye and nose. When the roses bloom this is a fairy-tale garden and one which is very enlightening. There is nowhere else where almost every type of rose and every centuries old historical group of old roses are so systematically organized.

There is a map of the garden on which the location of every type of rose is indicated, so that everyone can make a choice, and the character and nature of the shrub or bush. The exact colour combinations that are planned can be located and viewed. Consideration can be given in the other rose gardens about suitable ground-cover plants, perhaps in grey and blue, like *Ajuga*. Choice of the most

Red roses require ample space so that their strong colour can then form a pleasant contrast with the abundant greenery surrounding them.

suitable type of paving can be made. In Britain paths are common between roses, which is certainly excellent in winter when the roses are rather uninteresting. The freshness of grass is a welcome change. It is also fantastically cheap, but of course expensive in time to mow as all the hours that will be spent on it in the years to come need to be considered. This is why alternatives have been sought for centuries. Brick pavers, flagstones, gravel, shells, and compacted soil are all attractive. The last three are also simple to create.

It is not possible to use much by way of weed-killer with roses, so it is a good idea to take all the steps possible to prevent weeds in the paths. If anti-root sheeting is used beneath the paths and this is covered with sharp sand, weeds get little chance. Large slabs also make it more difficult for weeds to grow.

At Walenburg, the choice is for crazy-paving – in other words irregular broken slabs. The result is a piece of whimsy, contrasting well with the firm divisions of beds and paths. Whether I would ever use it in a garden, though, I doubt. But then people visit gardens to get new ideas, different notions from their own, and the rose garden at Walenburg is successful in offering these. If you are able to visit, check the open days first by telephoning the Dutch Garden Foundation in Amsterdam (++31-20-623 5058).

By adding sage, chicory, and fennel to a garden such as this, a pretty garden can also become a useful garden.

Perennials which flower all summer

Generations of gardeners in the past and gardeners today escape to the certainty of colour and abundant flowering offered by annuals and modern roses.

Around the bend in the path is a small border and then a substantial one, filled with yellow-flowering perennials.

Both groups of plants of course guarantee flowering throughout summer, lasting virtually until the onset of winter. There are fewer perennials that bloom continuously for months on end. However, there are some perennials that flower relatively longer than the majority and some which bloom again. *Acanthus* flowers endlessly and remains absorbing in autumn and winter with its long stems on which magenta cupped flowers are replaced by black fruits.

Achillea can also be made to continue to bloom if the dead flowers are cut right back to encourage new growth, which will flower until summer's end. *Aconitum*, an early flowering wild plant, is available in continued-flowering varieties such as *napellus*, which blooms well into autumn from summer, and there is also the white *napellus* 'Album', which grows to 80cm (32in). *Agastache* bears purple whorls of flowers for quite some time and attracts the bees and butterflies. *Alchemilla* should be cut back fully just after the peak of blooming, New foliage then appears, together with a second flowering. *Anaphalis* flowers throughout the summer and autumn in shades of white or pale yellow. It is mainly of dwarf habit, although some grow to 70cm (28in) – such as *margaritacea yedoensis*. Michaelmas daisies, *Aster*, are renowned for autumn flowers, but they can also bloom in summer. This is also true of *Astilbe*, but it is uncertain whether dead-heading helps with this. *Astrantia*, or masterwort, certainly continues to produce flowers if you make the

effort to remove dying flowers. *Calamintha* is essential for any gardener who wants long periods of flowering. It is a delightful, unassuming, misty hued plant with superbly scented leaves for tea and pot pourri. Turning to *Campanula*, there are those which flower for long periods, particularly the dwarf varieties such as *carpatica* and *portenschlagiana*. The taller ones certainly flower again if cut back to the first leaf. *Centranthus* blooms only once, except for the brick-red and white varieties. Take the trouble to remove wilting blooms though, and they will flower again. This can be done just beneath the flowers, with the shears, or by removing each flower as it finishes. *Cephalaria* is a spectacular plant growing effortlessly to 2m (6ft), with light yellow flowers similar to scabious. On clay soils they remain shorter. They flower from summer well into autumn. *Cimicifuga* or bugbane will flower from late summer until the first snow. The mauve-purple-leafed variety is *C. ramosa* 'Atropurpurea.'

Clematis is known as a climber but it is also available as a shrub. *Clematis recta* bears masses of white star-like flowers and can reach 2m (6ft), although it is generally lower. There are many light and dark blue shrub *Clematis*. For strong butter yellow there is *Coreopsis verticillata* whilst *C. verticillata* 'Moonbeam' is lemon-yellow, refined, and flowers throughout the summer well into autumn. *Delphinium* should be cut back rigorously to the ground

Honeysuckle is trained to a stake, beneath is the blue foliage of Hosta sieboldiana *'Elegans', which flowers mauve-white.*

TOWN GARDENS

Lavatera 'Barnsley' flowers non-stop for months on end.

after the first flowering, There is then a strong second show of flowers. The annual, larkspur, blooms the entire summer and autumn. *Dicentra* flowers perpetually, if *D. eximia* or *D. eximia* 'Alba' varieties are chosen. The first has pink flowers, 'Alba' is white. *Erigeron* blooms throughout autumn; *Eryngium* or sea holly does likewise; and also *Eupatorium*, which has huge architectural foliage on tall thin stems. *Euphorbia* is an irreplaceable plant for its spectacular variety of silver-grey, blue-grey, deep red and green-brown foliage. *Foeniculum* (fennel) is another plant which has a long flowering season, and a wonder plant that everyone should try is *Gaura*, which has long thin stems. These are very becoming when covered in a superabundance of flowers like masses of butterflies from summer until late autumn. *Geranium* varieties generally tend to have lengthy flowering periods, so choose a favourite colour and cut them back after flowering. This can be severe but need not be necessary. *G. macrorrhizum* will only flower once so leave it undisturbed. *Gillenia* blooms perpetually, with star-formed white labiate flowers. *Gypsophila* and *Helianthemum* were both popular with our grandparents for their long flowering season. The low rock rose comes in every imaginable colour, including a white, 'The Bride', which has grey foliage. *Heuchera* has rather gaunt little white flowers that seem to go on for ever on cobweb-fine stems. It is often planted for the foliage, which is sometimes green or purple in the case of

The warmth of stone and moisture provides an ideal place for seeds to germinate between the joints of setts, stone slabs, and pavers. Alchemilla seedlings can be seen.

There are many clerics' houses close to Salisbury Cathedral, in Britain, with lavender planted along the path to the front door. Cut them back with hedge shears in March–April to maintain vigorous flowering.

H. micrantha 'Palace Purple.' *Hyssopus* flowers for at least two months with blue flower masses on each green stem. This pretty woodland plant also has pink and white varieties. *Knautia* flowers perpetually with purple blooms that are similar to scabious. *Lamium* has two to three flowering flushes from May to the end of summer. *Lavatera* is popular with gardeners with no self control for continuous colour. The branches are graceful with a flower here and there. They bring a rarefied style to the border. *Lysimachia ephemerum* has greyish, elongated, and fine white star-shaped flowers which form an ear. It blooms for a considerable period and its foliage retains interest when flowering has ceased. *Mentha* (mint) causes no great excitement when it flowers but provides a mist of pleasant colour for the second half of the summer, into late autumn. It is delicious with tea. *Monarda*, or bergamot, is strong and flowers endlessly. Leave the dead flower clusters to attract birds. *Nepeta* or catmint is popular because it does not stop flowering throughout the summer. There are tall varieties such as *N. sibirica*, which grows to 90cm (36in). *Oenothera* comes in shades of yellow and there is an apricot-coloured evening primrose, *Oenothera* 'Apricot', which grows to 80cm (32in).

Origanum or dittany has a long flowering period and is still a jewel in the garden after blooming. There are numerous new taller and

Daylilies or Hemercallis are sturdy and thrive everywhere. They can be found in colours ranging from brown through yellow to purple.

dwarf varieties in deep purple, which are very collectable. These irresistible yet modest plants never bore. *Phlox* is another old-time favourite which is still popular. The brighter colours are still available but more subtle shades have been added such as *P. paniculata-hybride* 'Lavendelwolke' (cloud of lavender). In common with other repeat-flowering plants, *Phlox* will bloom again provided it is dead-headed. Remove half of the top shoots at the end of May to enjoy both early and mid-season flowering. *Polygonum* is queen of the long-flowering plants. The dwarf varieties are now out of fashion. Taller species such as *P. amplexicaule* have varieties which are pink to magenta. *Rudbeckia* produces flowers in shades of yellow that can be relied upon for colour for several months. Their inward pointed petals garland the brown cone at the flower's centre which gives the plant its common name, coneflower. *Salvia* flowers almost perpetually if dead flowers are removed. *Scabiosa* has clusters of flowers like tiny parasols of white or pale blue, dark blue, or pink, from summer to autumn. *Scutellaria incana* bears blue labiate flowers in clusters well through the summer. *Sedum* is always fascinating, firstly for its foliage and later for the young flower clusters. Hybrid genus *Solidaster* looks like both *Gypsophila* and golden rod with which it is crossed (*Solidago* x *Aster*). It is first class for misty effects, although strongly coloured, which is perishable these days. *Teucrium* is a sub-shrub and shrub, like lavender. It flowers all

This city-centre garden has sturdy plants capable of surviving slugs, damp, drought, and shade. Here with yellow candle-like flower spikes Lysimachia punctata *is combined on the right with* Hydrangea.

summer long into autumn with pink bells on stems and foliage of grey. There are pale yellow varieties growing to 70cm (28in), such as *T. scorodonia*. *Thalictrum* is a wonderfully elegant flowering family, consisting mainly of small blooms on open stems, generally in shades of purple, which flower late into autumn. *Tiarella wherryi* has white ears that flower perpetually on felty green leaves.

Verbascum can be relied upon for colour over a lengthy period with a choice of white, yellow, pale yellow, apricot, and pink flowers. These must be removed as the blooms die for flowering from summer until autumn. Deal with the dwarf and taller varieties of *Veronica* in the same way. Viola, better known as the pansy should not be ignored in the hunt for continuous colour. They flower without signs of weariness until the first snow, when they take a well-earned rest.

Lengthy flowering   Choose plants from the families mentioned in this chapter for continuous displays of colour, With many of these plants, it is important to remove dead flower heads to prevent them setting seed. This is time consuming and may involve drastic action with larkspur, lady's mantle, and some of the *Geranium* species. Visit gardens open to the public for ideas on perpetual flowering schemes.

This town-centre garden has bright red Astilbe 'Fanal' alongside the strong yellow of Lysimachia punctata.

Beautiful ways with climbers

Town gardens often need camouflage, a special eye-catcher perhaps, or a change from the sea of foliage and flowers. If there is an unsightly wall in the garden which cannot be improved then climbers could be the answer.

Ivy and evergreen honeysuckle are both plants that stay green all year and draw the eye. There are disadvantages to them as well as benefits, so choose carefully.

Actinidia This climber is not well known, except perhaps for *Actinidia kolomikta*. Once successfully established it climbs strongly to reach 2m (6ft) quickly, but it can go much higher if permitted. Its attraction is the way the leaves change colour from green to creamy white and pink. This alone is reason enough to train it as covering for an unattractive fence or wall, or to let it climb up a tree. Perhaps they are not common because there are no spectacular flowers, yet when combined with a climbing rose like 'Zepherine Drouhin' or a purple-hued decorative grapevine, they are a sophisticated delight.

Another *Actinidia* which is slowly coming into wider use in gardens, is the kiwi fruit, or Chinese gooseberry.

It is essential to plant both male and female plants together. The foliage of this plant of New Zealand origin, which is grey underneath and green on top, is rough and hairy. The flowers are creamy-white and the fruits of course have become known as the dark

Wisteria is a rampant climber, not to be trained up drain pipes or brittle fences because the stem will easily bend or fracture them. A strong steel cable is the best support.

brown edible delicacy. This species' name is *Actinidia chinensis* and a variety which crops quickly and heavily is 'Buitenpost.' This is an almost untameable climber that has an impressive rate of growth. Once the garlands of new shoots begin, kiwi fruit can be enjoyed for several months. Be aware that this plant grows rapidly and gets everywhere.

Akebia or chocolate vine

The flowers from this fine-leafed climber may not be as noticeable as Virginia creeper, climbing roses, or clematis, but there is something both wild and precious about the clusters which together form a cup that will beg attention when trained over an arch, along a pergola, or against a wall.

They flower fairly early, in May to June. The leaves are like the fingers of a hand with five small leaflets.

To enjoy the delicate features, plant Akebia along a path or close to seating. Only the mass of bright green foliage can be seen at a distance. Close up, the purple flowers can also be enjoyed.

This is a climber that is suitable for pergolas, roofs, and walls. It combines well with blue larkspur and also with lilac-pink *Chelone obliqua* or turtle-head.

Aristolochia or birthwort   This large-leafed climber has broad oval, green leaves, of at least 25cm (10in) circumference.

A. macrophylla grows strongly and is a decoration that is well worth considering for Art Deco houses. This attention-grabbing plant can also always be relied upon to embellish a none too exciting wall, gateway, or fence.

The interest is in the bright green foliage rather than the lip-shaped flowers. This plant is all in all an attractive feature with a touch of nostalgia.

Campsis   Also known as trumpet creeper, trumpet honeysuckle, or trumpet vine, this is a Mediterranean climber that is slowly gaining acceptance in gardens further afield, though it is perhaps not recognized by many gardeners.

The common name comes from the clusters of trumpet-form flowers. It has fine leaves and long shoots which are rampant against walls and also suitable for strongly made pergolas. Colours available range widely. The choices are from orange through yellow to white.

Celastrus scandens   The American bittersweet or staff tree is a prodigious climber, which once established can climb to an impressive height. It has oval leaves, but the real attraction of this plant is the brown fruits which split open to reveal orange seeds. These can be used decoratively in the home.

Clematis   Clematis is an enormous favourite, grown in countless countries in many varieties. Following are some clematis that do well in town gardens. It is important to remember that they generally need a sunny position with some screening from the full midday heat. Some varieties tolerate shade, so the beautiful stars can be enjoyed even in shady gardens.

Ivy creeps as readily as it climbs, making it one of the most popular ground-cover plants in the gardener's collection.

C. alpina is a surprise because of its large blue flowers borne in April to May ahead of most perennials. Tendrils grow 2 to 3m (6 to 10ft). *C. alpina* 'Pamela Jackman' is light blue, whilst 'Ruby', not surprisingly, is a soft red. Lovers of white choose *C. alpina* var. *sibirica* which can cope with cold winters.

C. durandii is a variety that grows to a shrub of about 1.5m (5ft) and bears blue flowers.

C. flammula has clusters of white flowers that hang like plums. It grows vigorously, reaching 5m (16ft) high if conditions are favourable for it.

C. macropetala often carries an extra wreath of erect flower scales at its centre, making the soft violet blue blooms appear to be doubles.

There are many varieties of *macropetala* for you to choose from. Popular ones include the following. 'Blue Bird' has very large dark blue flowers, between April and May. 'Rosy O'Grady' is pale pink. 'White Swan' is white. Both 'Rosy O'Grady' and 'White Swan' have large flowers.

Clematis montana is the most widely planted spring climber. It is to be seen climbing up houses, across pergolas, and over roofs everywhere with its luxuriant display of fairly small pink stars. The beautiful flower can even be enjoyed in shaded gardens. *C. montana* 'Tetrarose' bears larger, dark pink flowers. All *montana* grow to more than 10m (33ft).

Clematis orientalis is less vigorous but easily manages 3m (10ft). It flowers in August, which is welcome, with a surprising yellow colouring. *C. tangutica* is another yellow which climbs 2 to 3m (6 to 10ft). It is a delightful open shrub, flowering for the first time in June and continuing for several months afterwards.

Clematis vitalba is perhaps best avoided because it will take over large trees, sheds, and shrubs. Yet it is very pretty on a long pergola or against a large uninteresting wall or ugly corrugated roof. Following the abundance of delicate white flowers, are attractive plumes and seeds which catch the autumn and winter sun like jewels. It is not to be missed but think very carefully about its position. If the space is too small, cut it back every year.

Against white walls it is sensible to use trellis which can be removed when the masonry needs painting again.

Ivy or Hedera *can be used as a creeper to cover walls or sheds.*

The most beautiful *Clematis* for style and simplicity is probably *C. viticella*, which bears small magenta flowers from June right through until the end of August. *C.* 'Lasurstern' is one of the larger flowering species. Its deep purple is ideal to place in combination with *Thalictrum*, blue *Buddleja*, monkshood (*Aconitum*), and pale white roses.

Among unusual colours are 'Lady Betty Balfour' which is violet blue, 'Miss Bateman', a white, and 'Ville de Lyon' a popular shade of purple. There are also rather vulgar colours so it is important to ascertain precisely which colour the plant is.

Burford House near Ludlow, western England

There is a museum dedicated to *Clematis* run by John Treasurer at the lovely Georgian Burford House. Built of red brick, one of the side wings has displays showing where these plants originated. This is China, North and South America, and in European woodland margins, to which *Clematis vitalba* is native. Photographs show plants in their original habitat.

The museum is run in conjunction with possibly both Britain's and the world's biggest specialist *Clematis* nursery. Many varieties can be purchased. To show how plants suit different settings, a huge garden has been laid out with water features, grassy paths, and many

Rosa 'New Dawn' is the strongest climber for lovers of delicate shades. Feed them regularly and avoid too much shade and they will flower perpetually until well into autumn.

unusual trees and conifers – all are given ample room to expand. There is also a fascinating collection of ground-cover plants, consisting of perennials, decorative grasses, and dwarf conifers. *Clematis* is allowed to entwine in shrubs, trees, and some of the more open conifers for a feast of floral display. It is also to be found between ground-cover plants with large blooms on top of other plants. This is virtually unknown elsewhere and is an excellent way to show them off.

Here is a garden worth driving many miles to visit. Almost nowhere else are so many walls as interestingly festooned with *Clematis*. Sissinghurst in the south east of England is another garden with good examples of *Clematis*.

Hedera (ivy) Birds eat the berries of this ubiquitous climber, dropping them here and there as they perch on a branch, wall, or fence. The seedlings mainly grow where birds roost, but the ground needs to be bare for the insignificant little plants to have a chance. They will not survive in long grass. Choose an area where there is no competition, or a wall, in trees or any vertical surface to which ivy's tiny roots can grasp. The large shiny leaves of *Hedera helix* 'Woerneri', which is closely related to the familiar wild ivy, make it a magnificent ground-cover plant.

Climbing roses send out long shoots or stems which are either allowed to hang in wild abandon or can be trained neatly on trellis. This is Rosa *'New Dawn.'*

Many special ivy varieties have escaped from being house-plants into the garden. They are less attractive except perhaps *Hedera colchica* 'Arborescens', which is pretty.

Hydrangea petiolaris The climbing hydrangea prefers to grow in shade, so a northern or east-facing wall is best. Its flat white clusters of florets make a dazzling display when covering a wall.

Jasminum nudiflorum, winter jasmine Winter jasmine bears yellow flowers which unexpectedly burst forth like little trumpets from bare green branches to provide a cheering note in the late autumn and winter months. It reminds us of yellow-flowering spring plants to come such as *Forsythia, Cornus mas, Doronicum*, and winter aconites (*Eranthis*). Winter jasmine produces long shoots which can be trimmed after flowering to form a hedge. It is also pleasant to let the shoots cascade over walls of 70 to 80cm (28 to 32in).

Lonicera, honeysuckle Widely found in hedges and woods in the wild, with a delightful fragrance, *Lonicera periclymenum* has a light yellow flower tinged on the edge of the calyx with lilac.

This wild species is a perfect choice for shady gardens. The tendrils are best allowed to entwine in a shrub or tree or to wind their way

A narrow passageway between houses was equipped with metal arches on which a grapevine is festooned, making something of beauty from a parking place.

through a trellis. There is a semi-evergreen relative, *Lp.* 'Belgica', which bears small flowers and has less scent. *L.P.* 'Belgica Select' has pale yellow flowers with a purple exterior. It is also semi-evergreen. A much appreciated variety is *Lp.* 'Serotina', which is somewhat lilac-pink with creamy-yellow on the inside of the calyx. Wherever planted, this plant is certain to make people stop to sample its scent. No climbing honeysuckle appreciates being placed in the full sun, so give them a spot in the shade. A great favourite because of its dark lustrous evergreen foliage is *Lonicera henryi* with its elongated leaves. For beautiful colour, choose *L. tellmanniana* for its fresh orange and round leaves. If honeysuckle is placed in the sun it will be plagued with aphids but perhaps there will be sufficient birds in the garden to deal with them. If not, you will have to deal with them in some other way.

These low steps divide the terrace and rock plants from the rest of the garden with ground-cover plants like Campanula portenschlagiana.

Parthenocissus, Boston ivy or Japanese ivy

Never place this against a house where it can reach the window frames. *Parthenocissus tricuspidata* is the most commonly found of these creepers, and is fiery red in autumn. *P. tricuspidata* has several varieties: 'Green Spring', with shiny leaves; 'Veitchii Boskoop', with somewhat smaller ones; and 'Veitchii Robusta', with rough, rather purple leaves.

Left: Mauve against red brick is possible provided there is ample blue and grey in the other plants. Here Clematis *grows in a fruit tree which has been trained against the wall. Pretty but rather unpractical.*

Passiflora

Passion flower or *Passiflora* originates from New Zealand and should be placed against a sheltered south-facing wall to prevent frost damage. The plant grows rampantly, requiring lots of space. In return for this it will reward you with abundant, exotic flowers in demure pink and purple.

Passion flowers climb well on pergolas and trellis. The white variety is 'Constance Elliot.'

Polygonum, knotweed

Be warned that this is a particularly rampant climber. The *P. aubertii* and *baldschuanicum* species are also known as Russian vine and mile-a-minute; the latter name should be taken very seriously. Only plant knotweed if there is a large ugly wall or eyesore to lose completely from sight. Once introduced it requires drastic action to remove.

Pyracantha, firethorn

This is an open shrub which grows wild in Italy and on Sardinia and Corsica, where it forms the undergrowth of natural habitats. The cultivated varieties bear heavier crops of bright orange and yellow berries.

There is little difference between varieties, although some are variegated and others have white-edged leaves. The yellow berry varieties 'Soleil d'Or' and 'Golden Charmer' were specially cultivated for their very attractive berries.

The dark stripe at bottom left is a small stream which divides the terrace from the flower garden. On the right is a tangle of Buddleja alternifolia, and a mirror set in the wall.

The plant can be grown as an individual shrub, used to cover an ugly wall, or pruned to conform to an architectural feature. Provided you do not mind the task of clearing up the thorns, they can also be used for arches, columns, or blocks. *Pyracantha* has ferocious thorns, as its name implies.

Vitis, grapevine   Grapes have been grown in hot countries to make wine since the earliest civilizations. There are hardy varieties, such as those grown in German vineyards, mainly for producing white wines. The white 'Van der Laan' is robust and has its own distinctive taste. Better though, particularly for wine making, is 'Boskoops Glorie.'

A popular blue grape is 'Rembrandt.' For wine making there are far better varieties but these are popular as table grapes and that will appeal to most town gardeners. Plant them in well-prepared ground, with plenty of manure or fertilizer and top this with some soil before planting.

Pruning grapes is an art, determined by the position in which they are grown. Train them straight up a stake or pergola pole, then cut the side shoots back each year to between 10 to 15cm (4 to 6in) and repeat in the summer to give the bunches sufficient air and light. This applies equally to any shoots running horizontally across the top of a pergola.

A well-trained Wisteria. Cut them back to short spurs off the main stem, each with four leaves, bearing in mind that the flowering buds are formed on these spurs.

Where grapes are grown against a wall, there is the entire space of the wall to be covered. Fix galvanized or plasticized wires horizontally across the face of the wall. Train the shoots along these, allowing them to climb higher each year. In the winter, remove the leading shoots. The two side shoots are trained horizontally to left and right. Other shoots are pruned so that the wall is eventually covered by the vine. This will need spraying against mildew and requires pruning again in summer.

For those uninterested in the grapes but wanting attractive foliage, there is the purple grape *Vitis vinifera* 'Purpurea' or, for a rather coarse but very decorative leaf, *Vitis coignetiae*, which is usually planted for its magenta colouring in autumn. It is perfect for large arches, against red roofs of sheds, or on dark-coloured trellis.

Wisteria This climber from China has a mind of its own. Make sure when you obtain the plant that the tendrils are twined anti-clockwise around the stake or it will not flower! Once it has flowered, it can usually be relied upon to grow well. There are various ways *Wisteria* can be used. The most widespread is to train it to decorate the walls of a house or outbuildings. Provided with a wire they will climb as high as could ever be desired and over the roof if not stopped.

Where creepers are allowed to cover white walls, then either ensure the wall is sufficiently covered so that any grime is not visible or train them on wires which can be removed when the time comes to paint the wall.

94

A symmetrical close-boarded gate with neat hedge makes a surprisingly picturesque and welcoming entrance to this garden.

Control them by pruning in the same manner as vines, with short shoots emanating from chosen longer branches. The flowering comes from growth which is a year old or more. Prune after flowering and again in late winter.

Wisteria can be permitted to festoon itself unchecked over a pergola or pruned to a main branch running across the pergola with short side shoots. Either way, there will be ample flowering. The best-known species is undoubtedly *Wisteria sinensis* which bears pale blue racemes of flowers.

W. sinensis 'Alba' is white. The trusses of flowers are longer with *W. floribunda* 'Alba' which is similarly white. *W. floribunda* 'Macrobotrys' carries magnificent flower clusters which are at least 30cm (12in) long.

Wisteria at Churchill's birthplace

The world-renowned statesman Sir Winston Churchill ended his days living at a large country house, where he planned gardens with his wife.

The result is a number of memorable garden areas. The entrance is through a small gate in a large stone wall. Once inside, the visitor is immediately confronted by four elderly entwined grey trunks. Together they encircle two paths which cross. The trunks are at least

Lonicera x tellmanniana has trumpet-like flowers carried on the ends of shoots. Beneath is the yellow Corydalis, *a wild flower which loves lime and walls.*

Next page: Those who do not like grass can pave the greater part of the garden. The green can then be provided by climbing plants and plants in pots and containers.

2m (6ft) tall and are of *Wisteria*. From them spreads an extensive canopy of this exuberant and beautiful climber.

Combining climbers

There are many gardens in which a large variety of climbers can be seen together.

By the tower of Castle Walenburg I have seen *Wisteria* intertwine most effectively with *Akebia*, combining shades of purple and blue. Both of these climbers could also be grown with climbing roses, perhaps introducing shades of white and pale pink. There are many other possibilities.

For gardens planted mainly with blue flowers, *Clematis alpina* makes an excellent choice for arches – combined perhaps with blue grapes and the eccentricity of old-fashioned, one-time flowering white roses, since there are no blue roses.

Consider how things look in winter when combining climbers. *Lonicera henryi* with its elongated shiny evergreen leaves unfailingly ensures winter interest and cover, with the added benefit of purple flowers and blue-black berries to be enjoyed earlier. All ivy varieties are evergreen, whilst *Lonicera periclymenum* 'Belgica' is semi-evergreen.

Impatiens glandulifera, balsam, can grow to 2m (6ft) and is ideal for the lazy gardener or for those who want a wild look in their garden.

Although it has no green leaves to enjoy, winter jasmine's delightful flowers and bright green stems make it a winter attraction. Its flowers shine like stars on dull days. It needs trimming back regularly to stop it becoming unruly.

Climbing roses

From China comes a rose called *Rosa wichuraiana* which sends out long climbing tendrils. It has white flowers. They were hybridized with *Rosa multiflora*, originating in Japan, to create cultivated roses and further crossed in cultivation to provide today's continuous-flowering climbing roses. These present-day roses can also be grown as shrubs.

Rosa 'Alberic Barbier' produces white double flowers and in mature plants can produce a second flowering.

'Albertine' originates from 1921 and has flowers of warm pink combined with salmon pink that reach at least 4 to 5m (13 to 16ft) and attractive dark green leaves that later turn slightly reddish.

Another white climber is 'Bobby James', which bears overwhelming numbers of double flowers. It too grows strongly, reaching 3 to 5m (10 to 16ft) and has the bonus of bearing many hips.

A clear pink rose with small double flowers in clusters is 'Dorothy Perkins.' A less vigorous climber is 'Excelsa', which reaches a more modest 2m (6ft), bearing heavy displays of rounded double light red flowers. Unfortunately these roses only flower once.

Ivy brings a touch of informality festooned over the arches in this formal rose garden. In the beds is Rosa 'Buff Beauty.'

Beneath this mass of greenery enlivened by the purple stars of Clematis *is a metal summer-house and the timbers of a pergola.*

'Felicite et Perpetue' is a small double rose with glossy leaves that can climb high provided it is given support, otherwise it remains as a shrub of about 3m (10ft). It flowers abundantly and is one of the oldest climbing roses.

'Francoise Juranville' produces scented apricot double blooms worth noting. This rose has dark red foliage but is susceptible to mildew, so is best grown on pergolas and trained over arches – but not against warm walls.

'Goldfinch' produces just one flush of cream-yellow flowers with yellow stamens. It reaches 3m (10ft).

'Kew Rambler' sends out shoots of at least 5m (16ft) with flat open pink flowers that are edged with lilac.

A beautiful rose is 'Paul's Himalayan Musk Rambler', which I have seen attractively displayed with its deep violet flowers festooning a romantic wooden bridge on simple arches made of reinforcing mesh which could hardly be seen. Plain metal hoops were also used, painted dark green after being galvanized to reduce maintenance. The stems are so long that they reach to the tops of trees. This rose can be damaged by severe frosts so for really important settings it may be wiser to choose a hardier dark magenta rose.

Many climbers can be maintained as shrub roses through pruning, though they need plenty of space. 'Rambling Rector' not surprisingly can easily achieve 4m (13ft) or can be kept in check as a shrub. The

Clematis montana *forms a marquee-like canopy over a seating area in this garden. The climber has been trained over a series of cables.*

creamy-white flowers look good trained over hoops with a sea of lady's mantle and then further along the garden two shrubs of the same rose. Another excellent rose for pergolas or fences is 'Sander's White' with stems that grow to 5m (16ft) bearing cream-white trusses of small semi-double flowers amidst bright green foliage.

'Seagull' is widely planted because it is trouble-free, disease resistant, grows strongly and bears white flowers with yellow stamens in profusion. Grown over a large arch or on a summer-house roof, it will fill the garden with scent from June to July.

'Veilchenblau' is the choicest of the old climbers. It is purple with mauve and blue tinting. Place it in partial shade to retain the full beauty of this romantic climbing rose. It will reach 4m (13ft) with its stems.

'Wedding Day' is a white climber that has a mass of creamy blooms but with delicate apricot-coloured buds that mix well with other flowers. The stamens are tinged with orange. There is luxuriant foliage just like the flowers and stems reach 10m (33ft). These are some of the offspring from the original China rose *Rosa wichuraiana* and the Japanese rose *R. multiflora*.

The occupants of this house can look down into the garden or walk into it down stately (and safe) steps. The irregular shape of the lawn is repeated in the informality of the plants.

Ways to use old climbing roses	These roses are best used in combination with other continued-flowering roses and with *Clematis* and honeysuckle. The short flowering season from June to July is a distinct disadvantage but the thousands of flowers hanging heavy and wafting scent across the

garden are sufficient grounds to find room for them. Such a place could be a rose arch where *Clematis* can subsequently bloom. Alternatively a pergola can have a number of climbing plants combined, including one old climbing rose, which may flower just once for about a month. Pergolas offer great possibilities. Leave the climbing rose in peace on the stringers and cut the other climbers back each year so that they first decorate the uprights, only entwining themselves with the rose on the horizontal parts of the pergola once the rose is past flowering. To grow these old roses against fences or walls they need sturdy trelliswork or sturdily fixed wires that can withstand the weight. Place other climbers which flower longer or later at the feet of these roses. Roses can also be trained into old fruit trees so that the flowers hang down like jewels on the branches. A lovely way to use climbing roses is to prune shrubs so that they are open to allow roses to entwine in them, together with similar-coloured *Clematis*.

Perpetual flowering climbing roses

Fortunately there are climbing roses which will bloom more or less throughout the summer. Frequently I place them together with old roses in order to introduce variation among plants of similar shape and colour. Do not expect to find any bright red or stark yellow climbers amidst my recommendations, because I personally do not like them. Shades in between have been planted by me with alacrity for many years, including some very lively colours.

Campanula portenschlagiana *has long ground creeping tendrils on which the blue flowers appear from summer through into autumn.*

Apricot is currently much in vogue and an excellent climbing example of English origin is 'Abraham Darby', which can spread to cover 2m (6ft) given time, or else may be grown as a shrub.

An almost pure pink rose, but for the merest tinge of purple, is 'Bantry Bay.' Provided it is grown in rich soil with plenty of humus and an occasional feed of horse manure, this is a trouble-free rose which grows well and flowers profusely.

'China Town' has large double pale yellow blooms.

Blush Noisette' is a blush pink rose in the style of old roses which was discovered in 1817. Its flowers are cupped and double and its virtually thornless stems make it a perfect choice for gateways, alongside swimming pools, or in rose arches. Grown as a shrub, it is about 1.5m (5ft) tall.

The climbing version of that not yet surpassed floribunda, *Rosa* 'Iceberg', has crisp white flowers which perpetually appear above bright green foliage.

'Compassion' bears peach-like blooms, combining amber, salmon pink, and light red – but predominantly amber. It is a robust rose which bears large scented flowers.

Another lovely white rose is 'Colonial White', whose creamy double flowers have masses of petals. It is a quartered bloom in the old style although first cultivated in 1959. It is richly scented and flowers twice in the season.

This cottage garden is planted with flowers that bloom in deep shades of purple combined with lilac and pink for a scintillating result. The pink is Astilbe, *mauve is added by* Phlox. *These are plants capable of growing well in partial shade.*

Behind the real stone sphere in this town house garden, Hydrangea grown as standards provide a feature visible from the house.

'Climbing Etoile', from earlier in the twentieth century, produces a deep red which combines well with light pink.

'Gloire de Dijon' is a climbing tea rose mixing tinges of yellow, apricot, and blush of soft pink in a delightful double quartered rosette which is a perfect choice for romantics and lovers of subtlety. It looks good against darker or buff-coloured walls and superb when combined with light or dark blue *Clematis*. It will even thrive in partial shade.

'Golden Showers' blooms firstly strong yellow then paler, which can be interesting or rather messy. It is a very upright rose that grows practically anywhere. Its flowers are open and new stems are somewhat brown.

This long back-garden has been laid out formally with low hedges of box, roses and in the foreground a small statue. The formality is surrounded by looser, more relaxed planting.

'Golden Showers' on rose arches at Giverny

When the impressionist painter Monet's garden at Giverny in France was restored, new roses were planted over the broad metal archways painted light green that span the main central path. The combination of perpetual pink of *Rosa* 'New Dawn' and yellow of 'Golden Showers' is an unusual combination, and there are lessons on the artistic use of colour to be learned from this garden.

'Goldstern' is a true golden rose, providing warmth and frivolity for otherwise sombre gardens with its large double blooms.

'Guirlande d'Amour' or garland of love is aptly named. It is much used for small hedges and arches or against walls or climbing through open-hearted shrubs, such as soft fruit bushes. Its blooms are romantic, small, and semi-double and they continue to appear.

'Lawrence Johnston' is named after the owner and designer of one of the most influential gardens of the last one hundred years at Hidcote Manor in Great Britain. The flowers are lemon yellow, scented, and semi-double. It has a less profuse second showing as a harbinger of winter.

'Leander' is a desirable apricot-coloured rose. It has small flowers, an advantage for compact gardens. Large flowers truly appear to overpower smaller gardens.

Another apricot-tinted rose is 'Metanoia' which combines particularly well with the small white-flowered *Clematis viticella*. 'Mermaid' is golden-yellow with nice open flowers. A delightful use seen in a garden is to frame a large picture window with the rose, which enjoys the warmth and protection of screening close to the house. Its stamens are very pale. It should not be sited in cold draughty positions.

'Madame Alfred Carriere' is a pale pink rose that fades to white. It is a refined and romantic rose which has a slight second flush and can happily tolerate north-facing walls and partial shade. Ensure the position gets plenty of reflected light.

A plain pink rose with a darker centre to its pompom flowers is

Apart from the darker eyes, Phlox paniculata *hybrid 'Mies Copijn', has pure pink flowers. Alongside is the pure white of* Aster divaricatus. *Note the edging between lawn and border which allows the grass to be cut without damaging the plants.*

'Climbing Madame Caroline Testout', which blooms profusely on stems that reach about 4m (13ft).

'Madame Gregoire Staechelin' is also known as 'Spanish Beauty.' It can make an overwhelming impression with its large, 15cm (5in), carmine flowers, beautified by yellow stamens.

Perhaps the most widely used climber is 'New Dawn', chosen for the strength and reliability of this bewitching pink rose. It flowers well into autumn, although sometimes only the first flush is abundant.

'Parkdirektor Riggers' grows well in northern climates.

'Paul's Lemon Pillar' starts with lemon-cream flowers which later turn white. A rich early flowering is enchanting as it covers a fence or frames a window with delicate, scented pointed to rounded double blooms. It has been chosen by many noted gardeners, including Vita Sackville-West, who planted it at Sissinghurst.

'Pink Cloud' is a vibrant fuschia colour which can liven up northern walls. Mix it with *Clematis* such as 'Nelly Moser' or 'Lasurstern.'

'Swan Lake' is a white rose which looks excellent blooming in front of old weathered walls. The flowers are double with a central blush of pink. Plant it in well-manured soil for lavish blooms.

A favourite of mine among climbing roses is 'Zepherine Drouhin', popular for its vibrant violet colour and thornless stems plus healthy leaves and perpetual flowering.

This almost architectural garden offers somewhere to wander peacefully surrounded by the calmness of almost total green tones. The formal pond may perhaps mirror the deep thoughts stirred in peaceful solitude.

Other ways with climbing roses

The English are reputed to have roses in every garden. Sometimes it seems as though these gardens all have roses climbing everywhere. What are the best ways to use climbing roses? Rose arches are back in fashion and they are simple to construct. Double arches linked together as a small arbour are very attractive. This provides space for a rose to be combined with another climber. Choose one that complements and extends interest, for example a climbing rose with an early-flowering clematis or wisteria. Whilst the rose is still green the other climber provides colour.

This approach can be played with as much as wished. More climbing plants can be combined together on larger arches, perhaps 3.2m (10ft) high by 4m (13ft) wide. With single arches of sufficient width combinations such as grapevine and clematis or climbing rose and wisteria are possible.

Bear the autumn and winter in mind when planning. For autumn, *Celastrus* might be chosen for the orange and brown when the seeds burst open. You can combine it with an abundant summer-flowering rose. Alternatively there are *Amplelopsis* and *Parthenocissus*, both of which have strongly reddish leaves in autumn. Honeysuckle too provides fresh autumn interest with its bright red berries that are enthusiastically gobbled up by birds.

Polygonum amplexicaule *is a recent arrival. It flowers profusely and for a long season with varieties offering dark lilac, pink, and white. On the right in the foreground is the liquorice plant* Agastache foeniculum, *useful as a herb. To avoid hundreds of seedlings remove the shoots after the long flowering.*

107

For those who like training shrubs, the yellow berries of firethorn can be trimmed to cover an arch. The berries will probably stay throughout the winter. Winter jasmine requires regular trimming and the heavy stems which are allowed to climb require firm fastenings to prevent them falling back onto the garden as a mess. If time is not a problem, and the small garden is not too demanding, then the plentiful supply of yellow flowers from winter jasmine can be enjoyed right through until the last of the spring bulbs have flowered and faded.

Imagine a clump of Christmas rose, perhaps *Helleborus argutifolius* (*H. corsicus*) which has borne yellow-green flowers from early December, on either side of an arch. At the same time winter jasmine which is trained over the arch comes into bloom. At an otherwise quiet period in the garden, this gives tremendous colour to enliven the winter months.

Simultaneous flowering for archways

Most climbers flower in summer, which is why they combine well with climbing roses. Honeysuckle is an example. In my garden *Rosa* 'New Dawn' pink flowers are one side of the pathway to our front door along with pink honeysuckle, *Lonicera peryclimenum* 'Serotina', which flowers fully slightly later than the rose. They work perfectly together. Within a couple of weeks of the first copious

flush of the rose, the first flowers appear on the honeysuckle. They continue flowering until the second flush of the rose. This is followed by the attractive berries on the honeysuckle. The new green shoots survive the frost without damage, giving great promise through the winter of warmer days. Once they arrive the promise is fulfilled.

There are also attractive colours among the varieties of *Clematis* which will combine well with many different roses.

All the deep purple colours of the small bloom varieties of *Viticella* can be mixed well with roses and also with mauve clematis. The lilac and pink colours are difficult to combine because they are more likely to clash. The best idea is to visit gardens where combinations can be seen growing together. A great deal can be learned from careful study of other gardens.

Combining climbing roses with perennials

The stem of a climbing rose is often unattractive and woody. This is why with rose arches something else is usually planted to hide the lower part of the rose. This could be lady's mantle, although this is probably not tall enough. *Crambe cordifolia* with its bold leaves is suitable to drape over the bare rose stems. One problem with many plants used for this purpose is that they are placed so close that they impede new rose shoots. Therefore open plants are preferable, or

Grey and green foliage is the connecting link to lead the way along this path of broken slabs and setts.

Santolina *forms large mounds and grows rapidly.*

you could place bushy plants a little further away. A suitable open plant is *Thalictrum*, which has little foliage yet grows tall enough, or the newer varieties of *Nepeta*, known to people solely for the edging plant catmint. This is of course also suitable, but taller *Nepeta* is better at the foot of climbing roses.

In England, many people plant larkspur next to climbing roses, aware that it will be cut back after flowering when the new rose shoots appear.

Where roses ramble up a wall or across a fence or trellis, the possibilities are almost endless for combining other plants in the foreground to make an exciting overall display. The best results are not achieved by mixing every conceivable colour together. That suits farmhouse gardens which are surrounded by endless green. In urban settings, there are so many other colours – of cars, people's clothes, and the different colourings in the buildings – that a more restful approach is appropriate.

Combining green foliage with climbing roses

Many *Hosta* have attractive leaves edged with white or yellow or blue. There are also simple, often bright green leaves which through pattern and form provide an interesting feature. Mix them together with other types of foliage such as *Crambe cordifolia*, and

This apparently wild garden is carefully managed. The abundant floral display includes roses which have been allowed to become small trees.

choose grey for the introduction of another colour with grey foliage perennials.

When combined with green the result is a restful backcloth for pure white, creamy-white, or pale pink climbing roses. The eye can enjoy the scene at its leisure. For a clever touch, plant lots of white *Narcissus triandus* 'Thalia', with, for example, snowdrops and yellow winter aconites. They become lost beneath foliage but will create a feast of flowering to enjoy early in the year.

Those with a very relaxing colour scheme indoors may want more colour in their garden. Some people intentionally decorate their homes with peaceful colours for both visual and spiritual harmony and repose to compensate for busy town lives. In this case the garden can be a greater jumble of colours closed in within walls and partitions but with the neutralizing effect of grass. A lawn provides a peaceful area of green which can happily be surrounded by a vibrant border full of violet, pink, and blue colours.

Alternatively a yellow border can be supplemented with blues and some grey mixed in. Another way is to choose just one colour – say blue, purple, or apricot – and then seek out colours which complement and strengthen the main colour.

This symmetrical town garden has a formal pond with round trimmed conifers at each corner. There is a border on either side of the pond.

Gardening with colour is just like painting. Too great an area of just one shade is boring and, as with painting, there is a need to introduce darker tones. This can be through darker foliage or deeper coloured flowers for contrast and highlight, to provide depth, and to act as backdrop.

The choice of climbing rose has a large part to play in this canvas. Choosing climbers with russet leaves such as 'Zepherine Drouhin' introduces tones to blend with darker pink, deeper red, and purple, creating a greater depth in the scene.

The scope is endless for experimentation and originality. Perhaps a climbing rose might be planted on its own slap in the middle of a border, trained over a metal pyramid which is painted dark green. In this way the rose can display the beauty of both flowers and leaves in all directions.

The delight of roses displayed in this way, or climbing over archways and along paths, is that the flowers can be viewed from close up and the scent easily sampled. It also makes them easier to prune, to remove dead roses from after flowering, and to spray if necessary to combat mildew and rust. Spray only if essential. There are many varieties which cannot cope with a hot, sunny, sweltering position

This garden is arranged in regular patterns. It also has lawn, a pond, and a vegetable garden. Even the vegetable garden is arranged decoratively and surrounded by dwarf box hedges and examples of topiary.

without displaying various leaf disorders. If things get so bad that the buds do not open because of mildew then many will resort to the most awful poisons to cure matters.

This is a slippery slope and a better solution is to select a site with ample ventilation and sun which is neither too moist nor too dry. Provided they are well mulched and fed, and strongly pruned back, then little can go wrong with them. Those with a sweltering garden will need to spray from the first appearance of the leaves until the end of the summer. Do this responsibly with one of the more environmentally friendly means in order not to damage the garden. There are simple solutions to hand around the house which are effective.

Simple remedies for pests and diseases

Plant herbs close to roses. Mint and chives help to combat black spot and mildew. If despite this black spot is discovered, remove the affected leaves and throw them away with the household rubbish. On no account put them on the compost heap since this will only spread the problem. For aphids make an infusion of stinging nettle and horse-tail, both of which are easy enough to find. Leave them a few days in a bucket of water before sprinkling the water over the roses. Repeat regularly and aphids should be no problem, nor should disease. Every good book on roses deals in depth with this

This attractive hedge of hornbeam, Carpinus betulus, *acts as an extension to the entrance hall. One item is needed to complete this scene. Fortunately, this avenue of trees now leads to an imposing statue.*

113

subject and there are also special courses on gardening without chemicals. Gardening magazines and articles give tips, so read plenty to become an ecologically sound gardener. These articles are often written by people whose livelihood depends on successfully dealing with pests and diseases. Put the garden sprayer to one side as long as possible. If it really must be used, then save the rose.

Accept responsibility for plants by ensuring they are properly looked after, in the right conditions. They are the boss, humans just their carers. This, as most gardeners know, is the reality of gardening.

Grass can be beautiful in its own right and need not be mown every week of spring and summer. Here Pennisetum alopecuroides *provides a haze of fresh green against the stark white of the house.*

This long narrow garden at the rear of a town centre restaurant is extensively used by diners before and after their meals. Large deep violet *Rhododendron* together with a very tall *Magnolia soulangiana* establish the main features and ensure that early spring and summer is truly spectacular. For later into autumn, there are *Hydrangea* and many delicate perennials such as *Dicentra*, *Tiarella*, and *Epimedium*. The terrace was enlarged and a further quiet place created for sitting among the huge shrubs, and for enjoyment of the view of an attractive outbuilding with its statues and ornaments.

A long narrow garden in which to eat, drink, and be merry

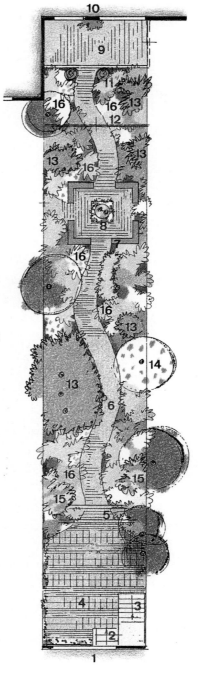

1 basement: large with enormous and very busy kitchen

2 steps up to garden

3 steps to the main building

4 terrace in patterns of brick pavers

5 masonry steps and also (not shown on plan) low masonry walls edging the planting at the correct height for seating

6 winding brick paver path

7 timber bench seat

8 ornament with fountain

9 large terrace in front of outbuilding in which exhibitions are sometimes held

10 outbuilding

11 box spheres

12 pergola with honeysuckle and a dark green archway

13 tall *Rhododendron*, deep violet

14 large *Magnolia soulangiana*

15 *Hydrangea* in shades of pink and blue

16 combinations of delicate low plants such as ground-covering *Tiarella*, *Dicentra*, *Epimedium*, and *Geranium* together with masses of bluebells and wild hyacinths in blue, pink, and white

Dark shadows or diffused light under trees

Not everyone is enthusiastic about trees in the garden. Many people have bad memories of sombre gardens but such an effect is both unfortunate and unnecessary. The correct tree in the appropriate position is beautiful.

Probe into the dislike people have of trees and it usually comes down to a case of trees that are much too large being grown close to houses, causing shadow. Even in the avenues in town, they are often placed so close to each other that not a vestige of light can reach the roadway. The lesson is to learn about their mature span and spread before planting trees in the garden. It is essential to choose both tree and position with care – this is presuming the decisions are within our control.

Look upwards from a tree seat into the constantly changing canopy of leaves. When the wind blows, the trunks can be seen to sway.

Small trees
Acer platanoides
'Globosum'

Acer platanoides or Norway maple has sharply lobed leaves in bright to dark green which interlink to form a tight mass. It forms a round crown for a perfect green parasol above a terrace or path.

Catalpa bignonioides
'Nana'

The rounded varieties of the Indian bean tree combine large oval leaves with a ball-formed crown.

It is perfect for gardens where not too much shade is desired. The crown is compact so that a hard but defined shadow is thrown on the terrace, plants, or grass.

Crataegus prunifolia
'Splendens'

The bright green leaf of this close relative to the hawthorn is attractively lobed at the edge. The tree bears white parasol-like florets which are succeeded in autumn by bright red berries, The combination of blossom, attractive leaves, and berries makes it a delight, especially when in early blossom.

Cercis siliquastrum, Judas tree

The entrancing heart-shaped leaves alone are sufficient to make it worth considering this tree. Since it also produces magnificent arrays of bright magenta pea-formed flowers in clusters on the stems ahead of or at the same time as the leaf buds burst, it is a must.

Visit the south of France in mid-April and mature specimens will be seen everywhere in full glory. They look best placed away from roofs with red tiles. An artistic French count of Noailles once laid out a garden in a former olive grove. The hillside in front of the house was terraced and a row of Judas trees was planted on one of the nearby terraces, trained along a pergola. In spring the roof of this pergola walkway is a magnificent canopy of magenta blossom. To train the Judas tree, prune after flowering to avoid removing the new growth, which will bloom. Never prune a short stem growing from the trunk because it will produce flowers.

Crateagus monogypa, common hawthorn or may

Birds have scattered this tree widely by eating its fruit. The tree spreads and bears the familiar mass of white blossom followed by red fruits. In town gardens there can be problems with caterpillars

For diversity in winter flowering species, an arboretum is a perfect place to find out about the many trees available. The winter frosts give added interest but do not normally destroy the flowers of Hamamelis, witch hazel, which bloom between autumn and spring.

and mildew but these are usually not major, so it is worth considering for a white garden.

Fraxinus ornus, manna ash
This large tree has a regular oval crown. The leaf is formed from a number of leaflets all linked by veins. The great masses of fuzzy growth of the flowers make the tree look rather like a giant plume of feathers.

Gingko biloba, maidenhair tree
An upright tree when young which spreads with age, this deciduous conifer bears fruits on the female which are orange. The kernels are edible but the fruits tend to fall and rot. This problem does not arise with male trees.

It has fan-shaped bright green leaves which turn golden-yellow in autumn. *Gingko biloba* is planted at temples in Japan where it is considered holy. They can grow quite tall.

Gleditsia triacanthos 'Sunburst'
This yellow-leafed tree, sometimes know as the honey locust, has small oval digitate leaflets on each leaf stem.

The variety is chosen for its small size comparative to its forest relative, *Gleditsia triacanthos*, which is capable of growing to 25m (82ft). Such a tree may take years to attain this size but sooner or later in most situations the owners will be faced with a shaded garden, albeit light and airy, or having to undertake serious pruning, perhaps even felling.

The 'Sunburst' variety has yellow-green leaves which are very attractive and a focal point for a completely green garden. *G. triacanthos* 'Skyline' is a lower variety with green leaves. *Gleditsia* is an ideal genus for creating a shade canopy.

Koelreuteria paniculata
This species is more often seen grown as a large shrub than as a tree. Sometimes known as the golden-rain tree, it appears rather thin and transparent from beneath its crown, with leaves higher up and trusses of lemon-coloured blossom which give a soft, hazy appearance.

Koelreuteria paniculata grows to become a substantial tree but it will not reach that height until two generations of gardeners have enjoyed it. Feathery leaves and delightful blossom make *Koelreuteria* an attractive choice. Few people seem to grow these trees as shrubs.

Laburnum
Probably the most hardy ornamental tree there is, in completely neglected gardens it becomes a large open tree that is both upright and spreading. When flowering, it is overwhelming, so surround it with soothing greenery so that it will be less overpowering.

For those desiring an explosion of colour, it can be combined with *Forsythia*, *Kerria*, and *Mahonia*. Finish this with an underplanting of different *Euphorbia* with grey, brown, and red foliage and the result will be spectacular – particularly if yellow-rimmed, *Hosta aureomarginata* is added.

An orchard can be a sheltered place in which to sit protected from sun and wind. In spring it will also be a sea of blossom.

Liquidambar styraciflua, sweet gum
The leaf, which is much like that of maple, is beautiful in summer and magnificent in autumn when it changes colour to bright red. Its leafless shape is also pleasing in winter.

This is ideal for those who like much greenery and are not fussy about blossom.

Liriodendron, tulip tree
This tree is much too large for small town gardens, but where there is sufficient space it is magnificent with its unusually shaped bright green leaves.

For lovers of spectacular blossom it is a true find. The four-fingered leaves are huge and the flowers stand erect like *Magnolia*, but are creamy white with lovely prominent stamens.

Magnolia kobus
These eye-catching trees which grow like oversized tulip trees are found all over Japan.

119

Wild trees and shrubs proliferate on mountainsides covered with azaleas and wild camellias. This is a delightful flowering tree with tulip-formed large cream flowers, which seem white when viewed from a distance.

There is only one problem with them, late frosts can turn the flowers brown. Shelter it behind a wall, with conifers, or close by the house where it is warmer.

Malus, crab apple   There are so many trouble-free trees within this genus that only a few can be mentioned.

One is *Malus floribunda*. This tree has delightful white blossom, which turns the broad crown into a subtly shaded but exuberant bouquet.

M. floribunda 'Golden Hornet' is more upright with rather less-refined white blossom and a surfeit of tiny yellow apples. This is more suitable for smaller gardens.

'John Downie' bears orange-red crab apples and is a much favoured choice.

'Liset' produces shiny red fruit.

M. floribunda 'Red Sentinel' literally swarms with dark red fruits which follow the pink-white blossom.

A single row of Pinus nigre nigra, *or Austrian deal, makes a year-round backdrop to this lawn and shelters the seat. When other foliage behind has gone, these conifers remain green.*

'Wintergold' is somewhat larger than the others at 7m (23ft) and bears yellow fruits which remain on the tree for some time.

The trees beyond the wall close the view to focus all attention on a fairy-tale garden with drifts of perennials in its borders.

Metasequoia These trees were discovered in the 1920s when found growing at a monastery in China.

The *Metasequoia* has been available again only for the past seventy years or so. Before that it was known only from fossil records. Then a living example was discovered, and through the cultivation of seed by Kew Gardens in Great Britain it has spread to become a common sight in both parks and gardens.

The tree is very upright and has an almost dead-straight trunk, which is rare in nature. The branches stand more or less horizontally and are branched at the tip. The branches are covered in needles which look like leaves, making this conifer a truly delightful picture of green.

This tree grows on most types of soil but its height can be a problem. They grow effortlessly to 10m (66ft).

Prunus, ornamental cherry The ornamental cherry is available in many forms, and the following suggestions are based on practical experience over many years. All

of this genus are very beautiful in leaf form, colour, and on account of their blossom.

A large chestnut shades Hydrangea in this formal garden.

Prunus 'Accolade' is one of the first to flower with its rich mauve-pink but tiny blossoms. It grows to about 5m (16ft), letting diffused light through its canopy.

P. cerasifera 'Nigra' is seen in countless gardens, chosen for its somewhat dominant red foliage. The blossom of this cherry is specially bewitching, appearing as it does before the frosts are ended, as tiny pink-white flowers.

P. fruticosa 'Globosa' has an oval crown bedecked with grey-green leaves. This shape together with masses of white blossoms is very beautiful.

Prunus 'Shirotae' grows to 5 to 7m (16 to 23ft) tall, and has horizontal branches and semi-double flowers of white.

A personal favourite is *P. subhirtella* 'Autumnalis', which can grow to 7m (23ft) and has pale pink blossoms that are almost double and nearly white. The blossom appears late in autumn as the winter frosts begin, giving a cheering display just as the rest of the garden is beginning to look bare.

Try to position it so that it has a dark background when seen from the usual vantage point. This can be a tall yew tree, a high holly, or a dark wall. Do not site this autumnal *Prunus* so that it catches the

Left: An older neighbourhood, where trees have matured and hedges are well established. Town can be truly green.

full force of the wind or the blossoms will drop prematurely, curtailing your enjoyment of them. Normally this is a fairly small tree. Lovers of pink will choose *P. s.* 'Autumnalis Rosea.'

Prunus yedoensis is my second favourite from this genus. Number one is the white 'Autumnalis', and close behind it is 'Accolade.' *Prunus yedoensis* makes the list for its wide-spreading branches, and prolific white blossom, and because of the horizontal growth of its branches.

Pyrus salicifolia, ornamental pear

This ornamental pear has elongated, slightly twisted silver-grey leaves that light up a garden. It is also attractive for its slender boughs.

The clusters of white blossom are similar to other pears but the green fruits are not edible. This tree creates a marvellous sense of spaciousness in smaller gardens.

Quercus palustris

The pin oak is far too tall for small gardens yet its horizontal branches are delightful and the deeply lobed glossy leaves are very attractive, particularly when they turn to red in autumn. In sufficiently large gardens, it is trouble-free since it can be grown in almost any conditions.

Catalpa bignonioides *'Nana', intentionally echoes the rectangular layout of this quiet, muted garden.*

123

Robinia pseudoacacia 'Tortuosa' The crooked twigs and divided leaves made up of oval leaflets are quite fascinating and the shape of this deciduous tree in winter is amusing.

Robinia pseudoacacia 'Umbraculifera' has a rounded crown which makes it popular for stylish uses.

It is so widely planted without problem that it must be regarded as trouble-free. To prevent this tree from outgrowing its position, it can be pollarded – in other words, you should cut its branches back to the top of its trunk.

Trunks of trees can be used as supports for climbers such as hop, ivy, Virginia creeper, and climbing Hydrangea. Hops clamber over ivy, already encircling the trunk of this tree.

Sophora japonica, pagoda tree Plant this tree in a large garden where successive generations can have the enjoyment of watching it grow taller and thicker. The blossom covers the entire tree in a soft yellow haze. The leaves are feathery and provide diffused sunlight rather than solid shadow.

Sorbus This is a trouble-free and hardy genus. *Sorbus aria*, or whitebeam, has grey-green leaves and red berries. When the buds burst into leaf the tree is illuminated with silver foliage. This is followed by white blossom. In summer, the oval crown is green but remains silver on the underside of the leaves. In autumn it is ablaze with many red berries and the leaves turn yellow. *S. aria* 'Magnifica' has a small crown and large shiny leaves with undersides of silver which contrast with the orange-red berries. The European native from this genus is *Sorbus aucuparia*, mountain ash or rowan. There are many similar species, originally native to other continents. All of them are easy to grow without difficulty. There is columnar 'Fastigiata, or varieties with red, orange-red, and dark red berries. *Sorbus interinedia*, Swedish whitebeam, is equally varied and each variety has its supporters. To make the best choice see the trees at a nursery in both spring and early winter. Usually the berries will help you make your choice. One thing is certain, with any of these there will be plenty of birds in the garden until they have stripped all the berries.

Taxodium distichum This conifer originates from the swamps of Virginia in the United States yet it thrives happily in less swampy conditions. When possible, however, place it close to water so that air roots will appear, after some years. The needles turn brown in autumn carpeting all beneath them but they are easy enough to clear up. Prune as lightly as possible, because the natural, upright shape looks best.

Trouble-free trees in the garden Everyone is glad of shade in a hot summer. This was always taken into account when gardens were planned in the past. Seating areas would be situated beneath old trees in deep shadow or partial shade from which the sun's rays lighting up the rest of the garden could be wondered at. A pale skin was then the epitome of beauty.

It is doubtful whether our forefathers new anything of skin cancer. Now that we do, it is sensible to have somewhere in the garden to escape the strongest sun of the day, however pleasant sunbathing may be.

Arbours Trees can be linked together, an example being avenues of limes which are often almost interwoven with each other, Arbours can be created by first pollarding trees and then restricting growth solely to horizontal branches. Two pollarded trees will form a natural parasol, giving ample shade for a medium-sized terrace. The height of these trees is not a problem, since upward growth is pruned back each year. The horizontal shoots will then intertwine. Positioning should depend entirely upon how much shade is needed. In siting limes, reckon on new growth reaching at least 1m (3ft). The principal problem with such an attractive feature is that of having so much heavy pruning to do every year, and having to clear away large volumes of wood. Four such trees can cover a large square to make a pleasantly shaded terrace. Place spheres or cubes of box or yew in pots alongside the terrace.

The same approach is possible with almost all trees that have a rounded crown. It brings a touch of the south of France into a garden. Place trees which flower early so they can be enjoyed from the

Without their leaves deciduous trees cast lines of shadow from the low winter sun, adding fresh interest to the changing scene on the lawn, by the pond, and elsewhere in the garden. In summer the beech, chestnut, and maple create dark shadow. Birch, hazel, and mimosa let light through to the garden.

house when it is bitterly cold outside, For rich white, pink, or light yellow blossom, a dark background is essential. This is not so for trees with more sedate blossom. Try to avoid having too many trees in bloom at the same time in one part of the garden. A flowering tree at the front of the house and another at the far end of the rear garden gives a very interesting effect. More formally, two can be placed right at the front with two more a short distance away but still in the front garden. This scene can be completed with hedges, holly, bamboo, or a fine leafed shrub such as *Acer palmatum*.

In complete contrast to the earlier orchard, these fruit trees are underplanted with perennials including Christmas roses.

Composition

The role that trees play in establishing the overall composition of a garden is an important one. Often a tree will rise out of a group of shrubs, combining to create a dense enclosed mass. For contrast, be sure to choose different form and colours of leaves when you are planning your garden.

There is no rule which insists that shrubs with red, gold, or silver-coloured foliage should be grown beneath trees but these combinations work well with the expanse of green of trees. Alongside trees with light coloured leaves, place darker ones such as *Prunus laurocerasus* 'Zabeliana', or needle-bearing conifers such as *Taxus baccata* 'Rapandens.' Place glossy or bright green-leafed trees next to those with matt foliage such as *Prunus fruticosa* 'Globosa.' With

enormous splashes of light green such as *Catalpa*, juxtapose a dark green shrub, not another bright green one.

Those wishing to enjoy the shape of the tree in its entirety should place a hedge or border of trimmed shrubs in the background and leave the tree standing alone. Beneath, place plants like *Hosta*, *Alchemilla*, and *Pachysandra*. Better still, surround the tree with paving, or place it alongside a path, next to a terrace, or in the centre of a lawn.

Trees are the ceiling to a garden. They are also the sun shades, and for the artist they provide both the frame and the height perspective for an overall image. As well as all that, they spring forth with their branches decked in green and may also become a blaze of blossom. To understand the size of mature trees in order to make an informed choice, visit an arboretum before calling at a garden centre to make your purchases.

These unusual shapes are the result of much patience. Peace rules in this endless sea of shades of green, yet excitement is provided by the play of changing light.

127

Garden of a large detached house The garden of this large detached house in a neighbourhood of similar homes underwent renovation. In other words, everything that had grown too big or was out of control was either cut back or removed. New planting gave the garden a fresh impetus. At the rear a floral festival was created. On one side, depth was emphasized with grass and planting, whilst at the front a stylish white-themed garden was created. Beside the long driveway the planting was better than ever before.

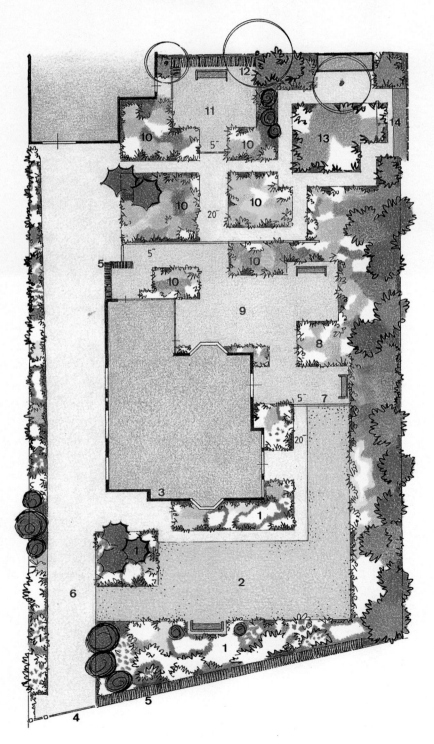

1 white perennials and rose border

2 lawn

3 front door

4 public highway

5 yew hedge

6 driveway of grey concrete pavers

7 brick paving

8 partial-shade border of pink-white

9 large terrace of brick pavers

10 perennials, roses, and shrubs in shades of pink, violet, blue, and some grey or lavender

11 new terrace with seating as eye-catcher

12 high yew hedge as backdrop

13 large group of existing *Rhododendron*

14 herb garden with trellis covering ugly wall of neighbouring garage

15 granny annexe with garage beneath and parking for cars

Partitioning with hedges and shrubs

With the increasingly small parcels of land that are allotted as gardens, it becomes ever more essential to surround the garden with a hedge to keep the tiny area as a quiet haven. This chapter considers the laying out of the garden.

The notion that conifers, shrubs, even trees such as beech can be pruned, trained, and shaped to will is generally accepted. A study of old gardens in the landscape style reveals that hedges used to be seldom used. People deemed them unnatural and considered the fully formed shape of shrubs, trees, and conifers should be admired. Looking closely at these gardens helps to identify some problems for town gardens. Left alone, shrubs and trees may well become breathtakingly lovely, but equally, many which look good when immature lose shape and become a mess in adulthood.

Pruning and shaping can be positive, producing a form that is suited to the garden but sometimes it can be excessive. It is best kept to the minimum. Knowing the growth habit of plants and the shape they develop to naturally is essential if you are to avoid strange, rather odd-looking gardens.

In my travels I have seen gardens with multi-coloured variegated-leafed shrubs trimmed to rounded shapes, regardless of their natural habit. *Ligustrum* and *Cornus* in particular are sometimes rendered unnatural and identical to one another.

This desire to force a personal whim upon everything without regard for the plants' natural shape is senseless. It reveals a lack of under-

Hydrangea is a fascinating genus. This is Hydrangea arborescens, *which starts as green, becomes cream, and then reverts to green.* H. a. 'Annabelle' *has even larger blooms.*

standing and knowledge of the way plants grow and develop. Once this knowledge is acquired, the urge to prune will be lessened, limited to a little thinning out and essential cutting back. In this way the natural shape can be fully enjoyed.

Hedges: when and where?

To avoid seeing the neighbours and to make the best use of the garden, some form of screening is usually necessary. Normally, this will be a hedge, trellis-work, fencing, or a wall. Of these, hedging is usually the cheapest. Privet, beech, and hornbeam are not expensive if planted small, at say lm (3ft) high. Privet is always planted as young stock to stop the bottom of the stem from becoming bare, resulting in a hedge "on legs". Many plants can be used for hedging, such as Portugal laurel (*Prunus lusitanica*), bamboo (*Sinarundinaria*), and Cornelian cherry (*Cornus mas*). Almost every shrub can be trimmed into a hedge. Some are bare footed right from the outset – such as *Aralia* and *Rhus* – but these are the exception. Where hedges are planted will depend on their purpose. For maximum privacy and as much space in the garden as possible, the hedge will be placed on the boundary of the garden. If its purpose is to partition off a part of the garden then it will be planted on the appropriate line. Dividing a garden up with hedges is almost as old as gardens themselves. In pre-Christian times areas of land were already hedged around, mainly with thorny shrubs such as holly and may. The herb garden together with the flower gar-

Shrubs can be used as hedging but then they will flower sporadically. It is better to place them as specimen shrubs where they can be allowed space to develop. This is Hydrangea macrophylla *'Bouquet Rose'.*

den and orchard was marked out with hedges to keep both cattle and passers-by away.

The town garden can be similarly sub-divided, into ornamental garden, herb garden, and, further from the house, the vegetable garden. The partitioning can be placed according to personal choice. Some may make an ornamental garden out of the herb garden. With vegetables that is harder, but not impossible. In a small garden it is best to keep all inner hedges as low as possible – no taller than 1 to 1.3m (3 to 4ft 3in) for small gardens or as high as 1.8m (6ft) for larger ones.

Gateways can be formed from the same plant as the hedge. This works well with beech, hornbeam, and holly. If your are using other shrubs an archway is best formed by training the plants around a metal hoop.

Separate bushes grown as screening
Many older gardens demonstrate how by cutting the front and back of bushes, an excellent boundary partition can be achieved. The standard combination in countless gardens is *Laburnum*, *Magnolia*, lilac, *Forsythia*, *Rhododendron*, *Aucuba*, and yew. These are all hardy and sturdy shrubs and conifers which without too much effort will grow into an almost solid wall. They do, however, have a tendency to become both broad and high, so that they are not suitable for the smaller garden. People can get to feel closed in behind them. This is

Those with little space must trim the hedge, as here. It is essential to leave space in the planting so that you can trim the lower part of the hedge. Choose thornless hedges so that you will not get pricked whilst gardening.

131

why I often remove a great deal, leaving just the most attractive plants, and possibly also cutting back somewhat to allow the extent of the garden to be seen. The spaciousness that can be easily achieved in established gardens by selectively removing things is astounding. For those who are starting from scratch, the variety of different plants that can be used as a boundary partition will probably appeal more than the less obviously attractive hedge. A combination is usually best. You could choose a length of hedge in front of a border, then shrubs and perhaps another hedge in the background, with trees standing high on prominent trunks. The alternatives to play with are limitless.

Shrubs standing alone

Prunus subhirtella 'Autumnalis' grown as a large shrub is ideal as a free-standing specimen. The shrub grows constantly larger and is continually pruned back to three or four bare branches with a clear view beneath them. This idea comes from Japan, where maple is always treated in this way. These silhouettes are placed in the foreground to create a sense of distant views beyond. This can also be done with quince, cherry, crab apples, and even hazel. The last will continue to make many new shoots from the ground which will need cutting back every year. Further back in the garden, the shrubs need not be so open to view beyond and it can be particularly attractive to have a compact mass. Plants ideal for this purpose include *Cotinus*, holly, *Escallonia*, and cherry laurel. When older, many shrubs become bare at the base. If there is cover behind, plants such as *Hosta* or even roses can be planted around the stem. To avoid having to do this, cut the shrub right back to just above the ground so that new growth is stimulated. This works with lilac, *Rhododendron*, and *Forsythia*. The procedure is sometimes called rejuvenation. It is best to remove some growth each year but not everything of course, because that would result in a unsightly gap.

Consider the winter scene

This is one of my own principal criteria for a successful garden. It must be possible to look out from the house and find much pleasure in doing so in winter because of plentiful evergreen plants. A trimmed holly, yew, or beech hedge is cheerful, together with spheres of evergreen and the fine tracery of branches of trees such as *Acer griseum*, with its white veining. Add the flowering of Christmas rose, winter jasmine, the miniature white snowballs of winter-flowering *Viburnum farreri*, and other winter blossoms such as Cornelian cherry (*Cornus mas*) for extra pleasure. Ensure there are tall open-growing evergreens such as holly, Portugal laurel, *Pieris japonica*, *Rhododendron*, *Skimmia*, and *Lonicera pileata*. It certainly pays to consider plants as winter features. This can also be achieved with the climbing ivy *Hedera helix* 'Arborescens.'

Gardening techniques and ornaments

The newcomer to gardening normally comes home with newly purchased plants, grabs the spade, and places them in an eye-catching spot in the garden.

Usually this works, but it can result in the death of the plant and cause much disappointment. People often unwittingly choose acid loving plants and set them in lime-rich ground, such as most clay soils. Plants such as *Rhododendron* which normally grow in acid soils cannot take lime rich clay or chalky ground.

Water butts or rainwater butts are ideal for those with house plants, yet with all the air pollution nowadays they are perhaps less valuable than was once the case.

Soil improvement

There are two possibilities here. If your garden is lime-rich clay, you should choose plants which thrive best on such soil or dig in a quantity of peat. Then the *Rhododendron* can thrive, since peat is acidic. This is known as improving the soil. Of course, it is first necessary to know which sort of soil is in the garden and secondly to learn which plants this suits or which will grow if the soil is improved.

Fortunately, there are a number of plants which will thrive anywhere – examples are privet and hornbeam for shrubs and hedges, lilac, *Laburnum*, and *Aucuba*, the standard set already mentioned. These are trouble-free plants which do well in various soil types to a greater or lesser extent. Don't even consider them. By limiting planting to these, it is possible to lay out an attractive garden anywhere. The many acid- or lime-loving plants should simply remain in the garden centre as far as you are concerned. Don't even consider them.

Better growth through manure

Since ancient times gardens have been enriched with old, well-rotted horse manure, or with the preferable cow manure. This was done to

For well-laid paving use good clean sharp sand or, if available, dredged river sand, to a depth of at least 15cm (6in). The main elements of the pattern are set out first and then laid, in this case in a standard bond.

feed soil, an important practice since year after year plants are grown in the same spot. This is still the best way of enriching the garden, and fortunately dried manure can now be purchased for spreading on the soil. It is both cleaner and easier for the gardener. Use it annually, preferably in the autumn when the rain will carry the nutrients to the roots.

Certain plants such as roses need extra nutrients. Once I had a lilac that failed to flower and was about to be cut down. My brother dumped a wheelbarrow-load of manure by it. The plant started flowering and has never looked back since.

When growth is poor and during flowering, heavy manuring can be beneficial. Plants can however be burned if you put too much manure in the planting hole. Be very careful to cover the manure in the bottom of the hole with earth when planting roses and arrange the main roots above this. It follows that a fairly deep hole is needed if manure is added.

Before planning a major improvement with manure or other humus, you should first have the soil analysed. Simple soil-testing kits will tell you the key points and a full analysis will pinpoint any deficiencies or problems. Whatever the diagnosis, the garden centre or nurseryman has a full assortment of specialist products to treat it. Some need to be dug in, others (the majority) are scattered – occasionally when it is wet, others only in dry conditions.

Read the instructions on the packaging carefully to avoid using too much, for that will result in the plants being scorched or making them grow too vigorously.

Watering

If a long dry period follows the spring planting season, then watering plants is essential. In smaller gardens this can be done in several ways. With large shrubs, leave a hose next to the plant for at least a quarter of an hour until the ground is really saturated. For large areas of planting, an oscillating or rotary sprayer can be used.

Certain plants are particularly demanding of water; give them additional supplies by directing the hose at them.

The outer edge is driven 20cm (8in) into the ground to hold the pavers firm.

There are many different automatic watering systems which can be set working by turning a tap or even pressing a button. These normally work with pvc tubing that feeds little spray heads. Such a system is not suitable for roses since too much water lands on the buds. For these the drip-feed systems are better. These are really just hoses with holes in them. An entire system of tubing can be laid in the ground with push-in extensions for watering specific plants. In this way water can be directed where needed.

When choosing your system, you must bear in mind the height of the individual plants. The spray head which must water a section of garden should not be located so that there is a risk of flattening a tall group of larkspur.

There are special sprayers for lawns which lift themselves out of the ground to work and sink back out of the way afterwards so that the mower can pass over them.

Some plants, such as yew, should not be watered too much or they will rot, which would be a shame as these are particularly long-lived plants.

Draw a plan of the garden with the different areas marked, and draw in with a compass the radius of the sprayer circles so that they just overlap. From this you can determine where to place the sprayers.

Containers, pots, and lighting

Plant containers come in a tremendous range of shapes, sizes, and materials.

Traditionally they are of cast iron, which is strong but heavy and can rust. Paint them dark green or mouse grey, which matches well with lead, zinc, and grey terracotta.

This roof garden for a busy young couple has black plant containers and dependable evergreen spheres grown as a standard plus evergreen shrubs.

Hanging baskets and tubs filled with flowers.

Many containers are bell shaped. Fancier versions decorated with geometrical patterns or with flowers are commonly available. You can put flowers in these and use the plain ones for planting ivy, box, and other evergreens.

Summer colour can also be planted in containers; examples are hanging *Pelargonium*, *Lobelia*, tobacco, perhaps with *Canna* as a tall centrepiece. The grey foliage hanging plants are effective combined with the yellow-green ornamental tobacco, *Nicotiana sanderae* 'Lime Green'.

Pots Pots have been in functional use for centuries, for instance for growing citrus fruits in houses where they can be brought on and protected from the winter.

Now they have become collectors' items for everyone. Some choose only straight-sided pots, preferably antique and without scrolls and flourishes. Others specifically choose garlands, fruit decorations, or ribbed sides. The choice is enormous.

There are simple Greek pots that are paler and more subtly coloured and also the warmer colours normally associated with terracotta. The most common are the bell-shaped pots which are broader at the top

Generations of civilization can be noted in Spanish gardens. People change and gardens change with them but the delightful old garden ornaments remain, such as this marvellous drinking fountain which has become a centre for flowers in pots.

than the bottom. Among the extensive variety are`baskets made of fired clay, which suit Hosta and the dwarf annual rock plants.

Apart from terracotta,, there are many other materials to choose from: stone, marble, lead, sandstone, concrete, timber, and various plastics. Concrete is not popular with me because the colour is usually too white but you can paint them dark green or mouse grey and they will be acceptable. The right choice is a question of the plants that are to be placed in them, unless the pot itself is merely for ornamentation and has a lid – in this case, plants are unnecessary, Such pots are usually of stone or marble. If they are wet and outdoors when it freezes, they will shatter.

At the palaces of Versailles near Paris, Hampton Court near London, and Het Loo in the Netherlands – and indeed in all other magnificent seventeenth- and eighteenth-century gardens – there are delightfully decorated garden pots to admire. Famous artists designed them and noted sculptors chiselled the decorations.

Lighting   The choice of garden lighting is in part determined by the style of the house. For a classical house, choose classical lighting; for the modern one, a wide range of simple round, oval, and rectangular lamps. The simpler the better is generally the best rule. Two of the same lanterns on a wall look more interesting than one. To light a path choose a

This summer-house is open to the air throughout the summer. In the winter the shutters are closed up to keep everything dry and reduce maintenance to a minimum.

137

lamp that blends with its background and directs light downwards. Many of the dark green and black garden lights are adjustable so that they can be trained on the path or to light up the plants. Bull's eye hurricane lamps look just right fixed on a square section pole. They are available in copper and in aluminium-finish steel. I prefer hurricane lamps to all others. Sometimes lighting is needed to provide form and shape and then the modern types are more suitable. Two lanterns on standards by an entrance are both attractive and practical. The glass balls that were once so popular have now been largely replaced by other designs.

Spotlights for evenings in the garden

There are plenty of black spotlights that can be fixed on a wall or in a tree and do not draw attention to themselves during the daytime. Some can be moved easily, others are permanent fixtures. However, if the intention is to see the garden lit up from within the house, then bear in mind that the lighting within the house will reflect upon the windows. Very strong floodlights will be needed to light the garden sufficiently to overcome this. Of course, if the lighting is for use when sitting outdoors then much lower-powered lamps can be used. Halogen lamps are cheaper to run than normal bulbs. Sodium vapour lamps are not suitable because of their orange light, which does not make the garden look attractive.

Lighting for eating outside

My town garden is not really suitable for outdoor living. The best idea for such a garden is to install electricity when the terrace and other hard landscaping is constructed. Then there can be sufficient light to read by. Lighting fixed in a pergola always looks really interesting. Either adjustable spotlights or hurricane lamps fixed to the uprights will do the job.

For a terrace deeper in the garden it is both pleasant and practical to light the path to it from above. For the terrace itself lamps can illuminate a tree or shrubs, and lighting for reading or dining is a good idea. Summer-houses should of course have lighting if they are to be used in the dark and here too the choice of lamps of character for fixing to the walls is huge. Try fixing spotlights in the summer-house so that they point upwards, giving a mysterious effect when they are viewed from a distance. Lighting can of course be quite easily installed on the house itself.

Lighting for the barbecue

Good lighting is absolutely essential anywhere there is a naked flame. With the types of barbecue that have a lid it is slightly less imperative but still advisable. It is important to avoid anyone stumbling over or putting a foot wrong near a lit barbecue. Another thing to bear in mind is that the business of cooking and dealing with the barbecue needs good lighting. The enjoyment of the food is undoubtedly enhanced if there is sufficient light.

Place lighting so that it does not shine directly into the faces of those enjoying an evening in the garden.

If the lighting is directed away from the house, an additional advantage is that it will be easier to see the illuminated garden when you are sitting indoors.

Holding barbecues in a town garden involves considering the neighbours. Some are put off the idea by the thought of them complaining about the smoke. The solution is simple: install a flue or chimney for the barbecue to carry the smoke away. This works well provided the neighbour is not directly in line from the prevailing wind. A portable barbecue can be moved to take account of this. Permanently installed barbecues are best made from brick pavers with matching paving. Do not use smooth slabs, for these can become slippery with splashed grease, and never use wood close to the barbecue.

Garden furniture of wood, metal, or wicker

The choice of garden furniture requires as much care as all the other aspects of the garden. You may prefer to avoid chairs and tables of white plastic or indeed of plastic of any colour. Choose instead wood which will weather to grey, or if the house is older you could pick romantic-style furniture in dark green. For the modern house an appropriate style is also preferable for the garden. Grey weathering

A wicker beach chair for two provides shelter and can be turned away from the wind.

looks surprisingly good on modern timber furniture. Place a large white parasol held by a wooden stand nearby and the atmosphere is completed. There are many attractive tables and chairs in metal of both traditional and modern design.

One eternally popular item is the French bistro table together with chairs in blue or white – or for older houses in white or dark green. Furniture can be painted or stained to match the colour scheme of the garden. You could complement larkspur, or blue *Campanula* with yellow roses. If you place the furniture next to a red-leafed hazel or a tree that has blossoms of a similar red, then you can be paint the furniture to match. You can, of course, play safe. Either dark green or white will fit well with everything.

Lazing in the sun
Lazing in the sun is very enjoyable yet remarkably few garden chairs are suited for the purpose. With deckchairs, the back does not get any exposure to the sun. The best solution is a sun lounger. This could be specially made and form part of the timber decking dealt with earlier. There are sun loungers to be bought, of course. These have adjustable backs and some work perfectly. Deckchairs are ideal for leisurely reading in the garden or sitting to talk with friends. When they are combined with footstools it is possible to relax fully in them if not to sunbathe. These traditional garden chairs are a pleasure to see in the

Deckchairs are nice for lazing in the sun. Ready-made cushions – available in a range of colours and styles – are just the thing to add interest.

garden. This is equally true of solid timber furniture. They can be eye-catching features in themselves, placed intentionally as part of the garden design,

Furniture suggests relaxation and involvement in the garden. Seeing the chairs in the garden makes your thoughts drift to relaxing there. In a town where the surroundings are turbulent, merely looking at a calmer place can instil peace and the chairs then beckon you invitingly to break off for a while for a cup of coffee or tea and a few moments' relaxation. In gardens I have designed, garden furniture is often used instead of ornaments – which pleases those who commission me since, although both are expensive, you can do so much more with garden furniture.

Seating alternatives Solid timber garden loungers that swing are a delightful option but a simple way to achieve both seating and a garden table is to use bricks or blocks with sleepers or timber resting on them. Benches and tables can be set upon lengths of timber sleeper set in the ground as uprights: the bench and table are easily fixed to them. This is cheaper than most quality alternatives.

Wicker Wicker is widely used indoors these days at many restaurants and other places to eat and drink. It is warm toned and rather romantic,

A garden in one of Europe's busiest cities. Gardening on a grand scale can be done in the town garden, as this large pond proves. The two terraces are laid with concrete slabs and pavers in a bronze colour.

141

and it is certainly much more attractive than white plastic furniture. Some wicker items can be bought quite inexpensively. More expensive wicker is usually reserved for a conservatory or by the door to the garden. If weathered-looking wooden furniture is used in the conservatory then a link between outdoors and indoors will be created. Try to find and afford good garden furniture. If money is short then buy some bistro chairs and a table and paint them black, yellow ochre, wine red, or magenta. This can make a big effect for just a little money. Be prepared to paint the furniture if necessary, or you can stick to hardwood. The latter leaves ample time spare for pruning the roses, selecting flowers for a bouquet, collecting herbs for a delicious soup or herb tea, or lazily contemplating the garden, your eye drifting from flower to flower as butterflies flutter and the blackbird sings.

It is great to be in town, for there you can find both good company and rest. Summer in the town garden, with all that beneficial shade – what more could anyone want?

The barrels on either side of this front door were painted white to match the house and filled with white busy lizzies.

The slightly sunken garden in the diagram was reached by steps made of timber pales. These were removed and replaced by attractive brick steps. Matching brick pavers were used for the terracing and paths which encircle luxuriant beds of roses, perennials, and a few flowering shrubs such as *Buddleja* and *Escallonia* 'Donald Seedling.' The garage-driveway was also added to the garden in phase two, when the car was banished to be parked outside.

Steps in the garden

1 kitchen
2 living room
3 terraces
4 new terrace of brick pavers
5 steps of brick
6 bed with white standard roses and box
   edging
7 lawn
8 steps of brick
9 bed with standard-grown *Hydrangea*
10 pink-blue plants with many autumn
   Anemone and pink roses
11 yew hedge
12 wide rose arch with Virginia creeper
   and grapes

Acknowledgements

A.J. van der Horst, Amsterdam: title page, pp 5, 6, 7 left, 9, 10, 11,13, 15, 18 right, 20, 21, 22, 23, 26, 27, 28, 30, 31 lower, 33 right, 34, 35, 36, 37 upper, 38, 40, 45, 47, 48, 49, 50, 51, 52, 54, 55, 56, 57, 58 right, 59, 61, 62, 63, 64, 65, 66, 67, 68, 69, 70, 71, 74, 75, 76, 77, 78, 79, 80, 81, 82 lower, 83, 84, 85, 86, 88, 89, 90, 91, 93, 94, 96, 97, 100 right, 101, 103, 105, 106, 107, 108, 109, 110, 113, 114, 116, 122 left, 123, 125, 127, 131, 133, 139, 140, 142

M. Kurpershoek, Amsterdam: p 134

P. Schut, Haarlem: pp 7 right, 14, 24, 25, 39, 41, 53, 72, 92, 104, 111, 112, 122 right, 130, 137

N. Vermeulen, Groningen: pp 8, 12, 16, 18 left, 19, 29, 31 upper, 33 left, 37 lower, 43, 44, 46, 58 left, 73, 82 upper, 87, 95, 98, 99, 100 left, 102, 117, 119, 120, 121, 124, 126, 132, 141

The author thanks Rianne van Bergen for her indispensable help in bringing this book to fruition.